WAITING & DATING

A SENSIBLE GUIDE TO A FULFILLING LOVE RELATIONSHIP

THE LEGACY & WISDOM OF **DR. MYLES MUNROE**

DESTINY IMAGE® PUBLISHERS, INC.

P.O. Box 310, Shippensburg, PA 17257-0310

"Promoting Inspired Lives."

This book and all other Destiny Image and Destiny Image Fiction books are available at Christian bookstores and distributors worldwide.

For more information on foreign distributors, call 717-532-3040.

Reach us on the Internet: www.destinyimage.com.

ISBN 13 TP: 978-0-7684-2157-6
ISBN 13 eBook: 978-0-7684-9630-7
ISBN 13 HC: 978-0-7684-1349-6
ISBN 13 LP: 978-0-7684-2976-3

For Worldwide Distribution, Printed in the U.S.A.
2 3 4 5 6 7 8 / 26 25 24 23 22

DEDICATION

To Charisa, my beloved daughter: You have made father-hood a pleasure, and I know that the principles in this book could only be credible because of your commitment and dedication to the values and moral standards your mom and I laid down for you.

To Chairo, my precious son: You have taught me the art of being a father by demanding from me the things a father needs to give his son. This book is not only dedicated to you but to your children and their children after them. May you continue to be an example of the values and standards we showed and taught you through our marriage relationship.

To every single unmarried person who desires the best in relationships: May the principles on these pages serve as a road map on your journey through the emotional seasons of interpersonal relationships.

To every parent who wants to help their children make wise decisions and keep themselves pure until marriage.

ACKNOWLEDGMENTS

N O ACCOMPLISHMENT IN LIFE IS WITHOUT THE COOPERATIVE effort of many gifted people who willingly and passionately dedicate themselves to excellence and quality. This book is no different. All we are on this human journey to eternity is the sum total of what we have learned from those who have shared their thoughts with us. I am eternally gratefully to the many teachers through the years who have given me the information, inspiration, and revelations to help me successfully navigate the uncertain waters of life. Thank you all for making me who I have become.

First, this book is the result of my own experience through the passage of youth to adulthood, and the successful transition to married life as a 25-year-old virgin. In this regard I would like to thank my dad, Matthias Munroe, and my beloved mother, Louise Munroe, who laid an excellent foundation in the Word of God for all of their 11 children. These principles taught me wise judgment and kept me from the many mistakes others have made.

Secondly, I wish to thank my beautiful, beloved wife, Ruth, for providing the opportunity for me to test the principles in this book through our own courtship relationship, and for helping me prove that God's way is still the right and best way to all successful relationships.

Thirdly, my precious daughter and son, Charisa and Chairo, allowed me to transmit these principles to their generation. Thank you for granting me the time to spend so many hours serving others and writing these books.

Thanks also to Don Milam and Lisa M. Ott, who helped guide this project to its finish, who kept up with my hectic travel schedule while making sure I stayed on my publishing schedule. Thank you for your commitment and constant support.

CONTENTS

PREPARING TO DATE

YOUNG PEOPLE ALL OVER THE WORLD, REGARDLESS OF CUL-
ture, share at least one thing in common: the challenge of
growing into successful adults. Every society has its own customs in this regard, certain rites of passage through which its
youth must navigate successfully in order to be recognized as
mature, responsible men and women. In Western countries,
one of the most common and socially significant of these customs is dating.

The word *dating* comes from the idea of "setting a date,"
where two people (or more, if on a group date) agree to get
together at a certain time and place for recreation and fellowship. Dating is an important vehicle in our culture for giving
young men and women the opportunity to get to know one
another in a socially acceptable manner.

Although dating as we know it today is not a Scriptural concept, it nevertheless has become thoroughly imbedded as a social norm. From a sociological standpoint, dating trends and practices indicate overall societal health, because the way people behave while dating usually reveals how they will behave when married. Habits and attitudes established during the dating years generally carry over into marriage.

As important as dating is in our society, however, questions remain in the minds of both parents and young people alike. What, exactly, *is* dating? What is its purpose? When is a person "ready" to date? What guidelines are appropriate for a dating relationship? These are important questions that deserve solid answers. Understanding dating is essential not only for teenagers and their parents, but also for older, newly single people who, because of divorce or widowhood, are re-entering the dating scene.

> Habits and attitudes established during the dating years generally carry over into marriage.

One of the most common questions that parents and their teenage children ask is, "How old should a person be before dating?" The answer is not as simple as some try to make it. In reality, the question of when a young person is ready to date is very subjective, depending on the parents' attitudes and the developmental level of the child. There is more involved than simply assigning a chronological age. Adolescents mature at different rates, and girls usually mature faster and earlier than boys do. Some children may be ready to date at the age of 13, while others may be 18 before they are ready. A person's readiness to date is largely a matter of maturity and environment.

Part of maturity is knowledge, and there are four principles or prerequisites that every person should meet *before* they begin dating. Knowing and applying these principles will help ensure dating success regardless of a person's status: younger, older, never married, or newly single again.

Three Principles of Dating Readiness

1. First of all, you are not ready to date until you are fully aware of both the benefits and the dangers of dating. Once you understand not only the perks but also the pitfalls of dating, you are mature enough to begin opening yourself up to more serious relationships.

The primary benefit of dating is the opportunity to get to know someone new, to build a new friendship with a member of the opposite sex. This is important for developing self-confidence and social interaction skills as well as for learning respect for each other as persons of worth, value, and dignity. At the top of the list of potential dating pitfalls is the danger of becoming physically and emotionally involved too quickly at too deep a level, leading to inappropriate behavior.

Human beings are social creatures, and we relate to each other on three levels: spirit, mind, and body. To put it another way, we interact with each other in the spiritual, soulical, and physical dimensions. This progression is very important. Healthy relationships should always begin at the spiritual and intellectual levels—the levels of purpose, motivation, interests, dreams, and personality. The physical dimension is the least important of the three, yet that is where we usually start. Our Western culture has completely reversed the process. Everywhere we turn in society—the media, the entertainment industry, the educational system and even, many times, the Church—the focus in relationships is on physical attraction first.

> Healthy relationships should always begin at the spiritual and intellectual levels—the levels of purpose, motivation, interests, dreams, and personality.

Young people today face great temptations and are under tremendous pressure from every quarter to jump immediately to the physical in a relationship. Physical attraction leads quickly to deep emotional involvement and the couple hasn't even had a chance to find out whether or not they share similar interests, dreams, or views on life. By the time those things come out and they begin to discover that they are not on similar levels spiritually or intellectually, it is too late because they are already emotionally entangled, making it extremely difficult to break off the relationship. Too often they simply plunge ahead with their emotional connection, resulting in frustrated and unfulfilled life dreams.

Before you start to date someone you are interested in, ask yourself, "Am I aware of the benefits as well as the dangers of dating this person?"

2. The second prerequisite for dating readiness is a good understanding of God's standards for relationships. *You need to learn or work out a clear set of guidelines for behavior based on God's Word*, or you are not ready to date. This requires a certain degree

of spiritual maturity. Waiting until you are in a dating situation to decide what is right or wrong or what you will or will not do is too late. Unless you settle those matters in your heart and mind *beforehand*, you will have little protection against temptation and could easily go too far. There are only two choices: either you will follow God's standards by deliberate choice, or you will follow the world's standards by default. Unless you plan ahead to keep yourself pure on a date, you probably won't.

Our modern society has come up with some weird criteria for dating. Some say that a person is ready to date upon entering puberty, or upon becoming a teenager. The only criterion for a believer and follower of Christ is to find and follow God's standards. If you do not know what those standards are or what God's characteristics are for a balanced spiritual person, then you are not ready to date. Dating is no place for trial and error. You should not even begin to develop a serious relationship with anyone until you understand what God expects and requires. If you are not sure, find out first.

> There are only two choices: either you will follow God's standards by deliberate choice, or you will follow the world's standards by default.

3. The third principle for preparing to date follows closely on the heels of the second. Once you have determined from Scripture what God's standards are, *resolve in your spirit that you will not lower or compromise those standards for any reason, even if it means losing dates.* Many people are willing to compromise moral or godly standards in order to get a date or to hold

onto a boyfriend or girlfriend. That is immature behavior and will cause a lot of problems. Standing firm on what you believe in is a sign of both spiritual and emotional maturity. There are no second-class areas of life to God. He is after your best. He wants you to obey Him, follow His Word, and stand firmly on His standards. Anything less and you cannot expect to receive His best.

Close attention to these three principles will help ensure that dating is a healthy and fulfilling experience both for you and for the persons you date.

YOU ARE READY TO DATE WHEN YOU DON'T NEED TO

A fourth dating principle, which arises from the other three and is the most important of all, is simply this: you are ready to date when you don't need to. If you feel that you "need" a date in order to be complete or fulfilled personally, you are not ready for dating. Need involves demand and implies that there is something lacking in life. The opposite of need is choice, which allows for a decision. A legitimate need eliminates choice. For example, if we need to eat a meal in order to stave off hunger, there is little deciding left to do; we sit down and eat. Once all our needs have been met, we are then free to choose based on personal preference or desire.

Consciously or subconsciously, the quest to fulfill our perceived needs drives our lives and influences all our decisions. This is just as true with relationships as with anything else. As long as you perceive lack or incompleteness within yourself, every relationship you enter will be, to one degree or another, an effort to supply that lack or bring a sense of completeness. If you feel deficient, you will build your entire relationship on that deficiency, because you will be looking to the other person to supply what you do not have.

Most people enter relationships with some sense of incompleteness or inadequacy. What they usually end up with is a weak 50-50 relationship. Neither person can give 100 percent because they both are focusing on what they do not have, which they hope to find in the other person. People in this kind of relationship live every day in insecurity, because they each are expected to supply the other's lack, and neither knows how long they can keep doing it. The relationship may last only as long as either of them feels it is satisfying their needs or compensating for their deficiencies.

You are ready to date only to the extent that you feel whole and complete within yourself, apart from any other person (except God). When you regard dating as a matter of *choice* rather than *necessity*, you are ready. It is a matter of your ability to be happy and content whether you are with someone else or not.

> When you regard dating as a matter of choice rather than necessity, you are ready.

Consider Adam, the first man, as an example. The second chapter of Genesis shows us a human being who was whole, complete, and content within himself and his companionship with God:

The Lord God formed the man from the dust of the ground and breathed into his nostrils the breath of life, and the man became a living being.

Now the Lord God had planted a garden in the east, in Eden; and there He put the man He had formed. And the Lord God made all kinds of trees grow out of the ground—trees that were pleasing to the eye and good for food. In the middle of the garden were the tree of life and the tree of the knowledge of good and evil....

The Lord God took the man and put him in the Garden of Eden to work it and take care of it....

The Lord God said, "It is not good for the man to be alone. I will make a helper suitable for him."

Now the Lord God had formed out of the ground all the beasts of the field and all the birds of the air. He brought them to the man to see what he would name them; and whatever the man called each living creature, that was its name. So the man gave names to all the livestock, the birds of the air and all the beasts of the field.

But for Adam no suitable helper was found. So the Lord God caused the man to fall into a deep sleep; and while he was sleeping, He took one of the man's ribs and closed up the place with flesh. Then the Lord God made a woman from the rib He had taken out of the man, and He brought her to the man (Gen. 2:7-9,15,18-22).

Before Eve came along, Adam was alone, but he was not lonely. Loneliness is a spiritual disease. Adam was alone because he was the only one of his kind, but he was completely fulfilled as a person. In tending the garden he had meaningful work to do. In his authority over the other living creatures, he was exercising his God-given dominion over the created order. He enjoyed full and open fellowship with his Creator.

Adam was so fulfilled within himself and so busy tending the garden and naming and caring for the birds and animals that he never felt the need or desire for a companion, this is called singleness or being single. He was so preoccupied with doing what God had told him to do that he sensed no need for a mate. Apparently, the thought never entered his head. Providing a mate for Adam was God's idea. Adam was completely self-fulfilled; he was ready for a mate *when he did not need one.*

It is the same way with dating. The time you are most prepared for dating is when you don't need anyone to complete you, fulfill you, or instill in you a sense of worth or purpose. You are ready to date when you have first learned how to be single.

LEARN HOW TO BE ALONE

Contentment with being alone involves learning how to be fulfilled in your singleness. A truly single person is one who is complete physically, emotionally, spiritually, and intellectually without dependence upon anyone else. Successful singles find their personal identity and sense of wholeness within themselves and in relationship with God. Because they are complete within themselves, only whole individuals are fully comfortable being alone. They can thrive and prosper whether or not they are involved in a relationship. For such people a relationship is an added blessing; it is icing on the cake.

A truly single person is one who is complete physically, emotionally, spiritually, and intellectually without dependence upon anyone else.

A whole person is one who has, first of all, a healthy self-concept. Many people struggle with feelings of inferiority and self-hatred. Such a person will have problems in any relationship. Healthy self-love is critically important to personal wholeness because it affects every other relationship.

Someone once asked Jesus what was the greatest commandment of all.

> *Jesus replied: "Love the Lord your God with all your heart and with all your soul and with all your mind.' This is the first and greatest commandment. And the second is like it: 'Love your neighbor* **as yourself**.' *All the Law and the Prophets hang on these two commandments"* (Matt. 22:37-40, emphasis added).

Our first responsibility is to love God with our whole being. Because He first loved us, we are able to love Him and, in turn, love ourselves in the sense of having a positive self-image as someone who is loved and valued by God. If we do not love ourselves, it will be difficult for us to love others, or even to relate to them properly.

Secondly, a whole person has a clear and solid faith. When we know what we believe and why we believe it, when we know what the Word of God says and are committed to obeying it, and when we have a good grasp of God's standards for our personal lives and are determined to live by them, we are well on our way to wholeness.

A third characteristic of wholeness is growing one's own roots. To grow your own roots means to have your focus of motivation and control within yourself rather than in other people. Many people allow others to control their lives. They dress to please other people, they buy what others are buying, and they think the way others think. Uncertain and uncomfortable with their own thoughts and ideas, they simply acquiesce to the thoughts and ideas of others. Whole people are self-motivated, internally directed, comfortable with themselves, and rooted firmly enough to stand strong and confident in the values they live by, even if at times they seem to be standing alone.

Being alone as a single person has many advantages, especially for a believer. One of the greatest of these is the opportunity to give undivided attention to the pursuit of spiritual growth and a deep relationship with the Lord. Married people, even committed believers, must divide their time and attention between spiritual pursuits and the everyday demands and challenges of married life. In his first letter to the believers in Corinth, Paul made that very point in describing the value of singleness:

> *Because of the present crisis, I think that it is good for you to remain as you are. Are you married? Do not seek a divorce. Are you unmarried? Do not look for a wife. But if you do marry, you have not sinned; and if a virgin marries, she has not sinned. But those who marry will face many troubles in this life, and I want to spare you this....*

I would like you to be free from concern. An unmarried man is concerned about the Lord's affairs—how he can please the Lord. But a married man is concerned about the affairs of this world—how he can please his wife— and his interests are divided. An unmarried woman or virgin is concerned about the Lord's affairs: Her aim is to be devoted to the Lord in both body and spirit. But a married woman is concerned about the affairs of this world—how she can please her husband. I am saying this for your own good, not to restrict you, but that you may live in a right way in undivided devotion to the Lord (1 Cor. 7:26-28;32-35).

Paul's counsel to singles is to use this time in your life to pursue "the Lord's affairs," to grow in "undivided devotion" to Him. Unfettered by the ties of marriage or other serious relationships, single people are free to concern themselves wholly with the things of God. Make the most of this time in your life. Learn to grow deep with God and to love Him by yourself first. Don't be in a rush to get into a relationship. Get your spiritual roots firmly embedded in God now, because once you get seriously involved with another person, particularly in a marriage relationship, your time and attention will be divided between that person and your devotion and service to God.

Work to develop yourself fully as a single person. Learn to be like Adam; get completely lost in God today. Become so consumed by God that He will have to interrupt you to bring another person into your life. Think of singleness as a blessing and a perfect opportunity for character development. You will have fewer distractions, a single-minded commitment, and a more open attitude because you will not be pressured by the need to please anyone except God.

> Become so consumed by God that He will have to interrupt you to bring another person into your life.

Learn to be an asset first. *You should be preoccupied with preparing yourself for whomever God is preparing for you.* Most people are so busy looking for the one God has prepared for them that they fail to prepare *themselves* for that person. Don't make that mistake. Use this time in life to prepare yourself.

True singleness is a sign of spiritual and emotional maturity. When you can be alone and enjoy it, you are a self-confident and self-aware person. You are well adjusted, not needing other people's approval to feel okay about yourself. It means that you have your act together and are ready for a deeper relationship. You have discovered and accepted who you are and can now truly give and share yourself with others. You are ready to relate (effectively).

SEEK FIRST GOD'S KINGDOM

Are you concerned about finding the "right" person? The best place to find a godly person is on the road to God's Kingdom. If you are interested in a spiritual person, look for him or her wherever the Spirit of God is. In God's scheme of things, we generally find what we need and want when we are not actively looking for them, but are focused instead on the Lord and His Kingdom. When our eyes are steadfastly fixed on God, He brings everything else into our sphere. Jesus stated it this way:

So do not worry, saying, "What shall we eat?" or "What shall we drink?" or "What shall we wear?" For the pagans run after all these things, and your heavenly Father knows that you need them. But seek first His kingdom and His righteousness, and all these things will be given to you as well. Therefore do not worry about tomorrow, for tomorrow will worry about itself. Each day has enough trouble of its own (Matt. 6:31-34).

Jesus said that we should not worry about our everyday needs such as food, drink, and clothing. I believe this principle extends to all the concerns we have in life, including our relationships and finding that "special someone." Our first priority as believers is to seek the Kingdom and righteousness of God. If we do that, He will see to it that we receive all those other things. The key is to fix our attention on God's will, God's Word, and God's glory, and trust Him for the rest.

> The best place to find a godly person is on the road to God's Kingdom.

Seeking the Kingdom and righteousness of God is like walking down a road toward a particular destination, keeping our eyes focused on the goal ahead of us. As long as we stay on the road before us, we grow in the grace and knowledge of the Lord and in His righteousness, which means knowing how to live, act, and relate correctly in life. This knowledge comes through God's Word and from spending time in His presence.

Along the way, various paths and alleys branch off from the road on either side. In those alleys stand people or objects that try to get our attention. They represent distractions, things that are not necessarily bad in and of themselves, but can cause us to take our eyes off of the Lord.

Consider a young man who is making his way down the road, diligently pursuing the Kingdom of God. All of a sudden, in one of the alleyways, he sees a very attractive young woman. Stopping dead in his tracks, he says to himself, "Wow, she's really cute! I'm going to check her out!" and then saunters over to make her acquaintance.

Two things have just happened. First, his eyes, which, a moment before, were filled with images of God's Kingdom, are now filled with the image of the young lady. Second, as he moves toward her, he will at some point step off the path because she is not on the road with him, and because he is not watching where he is going. It's like learning to ride a bicycle. Unless you keep your eyes straight ahead, the bicycle will not go straight; it will swerve to the left or right and throw you off balance. Once the young man lets his eyes wander to the alley, he will veer off the path, losing sight of God in the process. If he is not careful, before he knows it, he will end up somewhere he never intended to go.

Anytime we start seeking people, we will be led by people. This is the dynamic of balance that God wants us to see. Once we become preoccupied with someone, or with seeking a particular person, we run the risk of losing God's direction. If we step off the road to the Kingdom, whatever path we take will lead us backward so that whenever we do eventually make it back to the road, we will likely be bruised and bleeding and farther away from our goal than when we began.

Someone may object, "But if I don't go looking, I'm going to end up walking this whole road by myself." That's not how the dynamics work in the Kingdom of God. Matthew 6:33 says that if we seek first God's Kingdom and righteousness, then "all these things will be given" to us. The King James Version says, "all these things shall be *added* unto you" (emphasis added). The Greek word for *added* is the same root word from which we get our word "magnetize." This means that, as we go along our way seeking the Kingdom of God, all these other things that we are concerned about will be added—drawn to us like a magnet. We won't have to go looking for them. Whenever we follow God's principles, we receive God's provision and enjoy God's promises.

Here is the point: if you have to go look for someone, then the person you are looking for is not on the road with you, not following the same path you are. He or she is not seeking the Kingdom of God. If you find someone off the road, you will have to go out of your way to find them, probably stay out of your way to get them, and then spend the rest of your life trying to bring them into the way.

Anyone you get involved with as a believer should be headed the same way you are, and if both of you are on the same road, at the same approximate place, eventually you will run into each other. You won't have to go looking. Stay on the road, focus on seeking God's Kingdom and, sooner or later, someone of like mind and heart will approach and the two of you will be drawn together.

Don't ever become so preoccupied by who you want that you forget to be who you are. Who are you? As a believer and a follower of Christ, you are a child of God. You are His possession, His property, His precious gem. It will take you the rest of your life to learn about His knowledge, His Kingdom, and His righteousness and, therefore, learning about who you really are. Righteousness means right standing with God. He wants you to know where you stand with Him: who you are in Christ and what you have in Him.

> Don't ever become so preoccupied by who you want that you forget to be who you are.

If you become preoccupied with who you want, you will lose sight of who you are. God wants you to become so consumed by His Kingdom and righteousness that anybody you meet will be, first of all, someone who is on the road with you and, second, at the same place on the road as you are. That way you can move along and relate and grow together as complete individuals at the same stage of development and maturity.

WALKING IN AGREEMENT

A man and a woman who find each other while walking on the road to the Kingdom of God have a distinct advantage in their relationship over people who enter relationships born in the alleys and byways. Because they are moving in the same direction with a similar passion for God and hunger for His righteousness, they are already aligned in a manner that enables them easily to walk in agreement with each other. This is an important consideration for people who are preparing to date.

To walk in agreement with one another as believers is a central biblical principle, a primary characteristic of godliness. In the Old Testament book of Amos, God calls His people to task for their idolatry and disobedience, and then asks a fundamental question:

> *Hear this word the Lord has spoken against you, O people of Israel—against the whole family I brought up out of Egypt: "You only have I chosen of all the families of the earth; therefore I will punish you for all your sins." Do two walk together unless they have agreed to do so?* (Amos 3:1-3)

The implication is that no one can walk together in unity and harmony unless they agree to do so. Nobody can walk with God unless they agree to walk according to His principles and His Word. Walking together is contingent upon agreement.

This same principle also has a prominent place in the New Testament. In addressing the problem of divisions between believers in the church at Corinth, Paul writes, "I appeal to you, brothers, in the name of our Lord Jesus Christ, that all of you agree with one another so that there may be no divisions among you and that you may be perfectly united in mind and thought" (1 Cor. 1:10). Unity of mind and thought—walking in agreement—is the kind of relationship believers must have in order to experience God's power. This is true whether we are talking about a fellowship of believers, two believers joining together in marriage, or two believers entering into a dating relationship.

For example, consider the case of a Baptist dating a Catholic. No one can deny the fact that significant theological and doctrinal differences exist between Baptists and Catholics. These differences will make it very challenging, even difficult, for this couple to walk together in agreement. No matter how spiritual they may be, or how much prayer or fasting they have done, or even how full of the Spirit they are, they will face daunting obstacles in their relationship as they seek to walk in harmony. It is not impossible—the Spirit of God can bring harmony of mind and spirit—but it is difficult.

One of the major problems we face today in our relationships is that so many people want God's results without following God's principles. They look for a godly return without making a godly investment. Everyone seeks success in their relationships, but many have little real interest in God's place in those relationships. It is completely unreasonable to ignore God's standards and still expect a godly outcome.

Walking in agreement does not mean always seeing eye to eye on absolutely everything, but it does mean being in basic agreement in the Lord. Paul made this plea to two women who were part of the body of believers in the city of Philippi: "I plead with Euodia and I plead with Syntyche to agree with each other in the Lord" (Phil. 4:2). Unity begins with basic agreement in spirit, which then leads to harmony of mind, thought, and judgment.

> It is completely unreasonable to ignore God's standards and still expect a godly outcome.

Spiritual agreement in the Lord is the basis for agreement in every other area. It is the foundation stone for every truly successful, productive, and fruitful relationship. People can share common interests, intellectual pursuits, and have the same goals, but without spiritual agreement, they will still have broken relationships.

The secret to perfect agreement is to agree in the Lord. Our fundamental agreement must be spiritually based, which then provides a solid foundation for agreement in other areas. The basis for spiritual agreement is the Word of God. Spiritual agreement is the first step toward the goal of any meaningful relationship: the development of true intimacy.

WORK TOWARD INTIMACY

Few people realize that the seeds of either success or failure in marriage are sown during the dating period. Habits, attitudes, and thought processes that characterize a person's dating relationships will carry over into that person's marriage. As a single, if you want to ensure success in your future marriage, the time to plan and prepare for that success is now, while you are dating. That is why it is just as important to prepare yourself for dating as it is to prepare yourself for marriage.

The standards for successful dating are the same as those for successful marriage. According to the majority of marriage counselors, one of the most common reasons for the breakup of marriages at any stage is lack of intimacy. Most people associate intimacy with physical or sexual relations, but it is much deeper than that. Those who feel that having sex brings them intimacy are only scratching the surface.

Intimacy is not an act. Intimacy is a state of existence in which both partners in a relationship trust the other more and more with their innermost thoughts. They trust each other more and more with their innermost wishes, dreams, and desires. They trust each other more and more with their innermost emotions. Intimacy, then, is the key to any successful relationship.

Most modern relationships, marriage or otherwise, fall far short of attaining genuine intimacy. One reason for this is because, in our distorted age of romanticism, manipulation, microwave speed and 30-second sound bites, we expect instant intimacy. This is a false expectation and can be fatal to a relationship. True intimacy takes time to develop. Many people try to take a shortcut to intimacy through physical relations, which always leads to failure. The first step to true intimacy in a relationship is developing a oneness of spirit.

Relationship does not guarantee fellowship. Living together does not guarantee togetherness. If two people are close together in physical proximity but miles apart in spirit, there is no intimacy. They may be in the same room but in completely different worlds.

> The first step to true intimacy in a relationship is developing a oneness of spirit.

Ultimately, preparing to date means understanding that the chief purpose of serious dating is to develop true intimacy—a oneness of spirit—between a man and a woman. Once achieved, this spiritual relationship becomes the basis of a growing third- and fourth-level friendship, which then becomes the basis for engagement and marriage.

I always say to people, "Don't marry your lover, marry your friend," because physical and emotional love are 100 percent chemical. If you marry your lover, you are basing your marriage on chemical reactions, which change like the weather. When you date, focus on the spiritual instead of the physical. Use your dating time not to groom a lover but to grow a friend.

True friendship—not casual acquaintance, but people who are joined together in heart and soul—is the foundation for all successful long-term relationships. The problem is that too many people neither understand what true friendship is nor have any real clue how to make friends or how to be a friend. If you desire a friend rather than a lover, and to be a friend rather than to be a lover, then you are ready to date. The next step is to examine what friendship is all about, and learn how to get friends by being a friend.

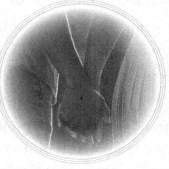

PRINCIPLES

1. You are ready to date when you are fully aware of both the benefits and the dangers of dating.

2. You are ready to date when you have worked out beforehand a clear set of guidelines for behavior based on God's Word.

3. You are ready to date when you have resolved in your spirit that you will not lower or compromise those standards for any reason, even if it means losing dates.

4. You are ready to date when you don't need to.

5. You are ready to date when you have first learned how to be alone.

6. A whole person has a healthy self-concept.

7. A whole person has a clear and solid faith.

8. A whole person grows his or her own roots in God.

9. You should be preoccupied with preparing your-self for whomever God is preparing for you.

10. Our first priority as believers is to seek the Kingdom and righteousness of God.

11. Don't ever become so preoccupied by who you want that you forget to be who you are.

12. Unity of mind and thought—walking in agreement—is the kind of relationship believers must have in order to experience God's power.

13. Intimacy is a state of existence in which both partners in a relationship trust the other more and more with their innermost thoughts.

14. The chief purpose of dating is to develop true intimacy—a oneness of spirit—between a man and a woman.

15. True friendship—not casual acquaintance, but people who are joined together heart and soul—is the foundation for all successful long-term re-lationships.

FRIENDSHIP-BUILDING: THE PURPOSE OF DATING

T RUE FRIENDSHIP IS THE STRONGEST RELATIONSHIP OF ALL, and is the fundamental ingredient of every truly successful marriage. Friendship does not come to full bloom overnight; it takes time to grow and mature. Since husbands and wives should enter marriage as best friends, it is important that they develop their friendship beforehand. Building this friendship is the greatest value and, indeed, the primary purpose of dating.

The strongest and most successful long-term relationships are those that are based on friendship rather than on any sense of need or incompleteness on the part of either or both persons involved. A relationship motivated by need destroys friendship because it is essentially self-centered. A person in need will enter a relationship seeking primarily to satisfy that need rather than seeking to satisfy the needs of the other person or help build that person's character. Entering a relationship primarily for what we can get out of it defrauds the other person, and that is sin.

One problem I have discovered through years of experience in counseling and from my own life is that most people do not understand how to build and maintain wholesome friendships. We don't know how to *make* friends or how to *be* a friend. While this is a serious problem among believers, it is even worse in the non-believing world.

Friendship in the world is based inevitably on manipulation. Consciously or not, people in the world use friendships as convenient and expedient opportunities to advance themselves. What the world calls friendship is not true friendship, because true friendship is based on love, which comes from God. People who are without God do not truly understand love and therefore cannot truly understand friendship.

When we became believers and were born again by the Spirit of God, our spirits were made new, but not our minds or our bodies. Those we must renew through knowledge and growth. The challenge we face is learning how to handle ourselves with a new spirit dwelling in an "old" mind and body that don't know how to behave. We have to *learn* how to live and act as children of God.

This is probably nowhere harder to do than in relationships, particularly between males and females. Our newborn spirits tell us one thing while our unrenewed minds and bodies tell us something else. Without a disciplined spirit, the chemical and sexual stirrings of mind and body are difficult to deny. That is why we must learn, as Paul writes, to "be transformed by the renewing of [our] mind[s]" (Rom. 12:2b), and to "take captive every thought to make it obedient to Christ" (2 Cor. 10:5b).

Many people ask, "How can I get to know someone without slipping into inappropriate behavior? How can I build a relationship based on friendship rather than physical attraction?" The answer lies first in understanding the nature and purpose of friendship, which is to build character, and, second, understanding the different levels of friendship and the behavior that is appropriate for each level.

QUESTIONS FOR BUILDING FRIENDSHIPS

Have you ever been in a situation where you wanted to meet someone but didn't know what to say or how to break the ice? That is a very common experience for most people. Few of us are taught while growing up how to speak to new people. On the contrary, we are cautioned not to talk to strangers. It is easy to forget that every friend or acquaintance of ours was a stranger once.

The key to overcoming this deficiency is to learn to focus on the other person rather than on ourselves and our fear or shyness. Getting our attention off of ourselves can help us develop a greater degree of self-confidence as well as help us learn how to listen more carefully to what others have to say. Focusing on the other person is one of the steadfast principles of friendship. Never talk about yourself; wait for the other person to ask. Instead, get that other person to tell you about himself or herself. Ask questions and then listen to the answers. Most people respond very favorably when they know someone else is genuinely interested in them.

Years ago, Dale Carnegie wrote a powerful and best-selling book titled *How to Win Friends and Influence People*. His first law was that we should never talk about ourselves but get others to talk about themselves. There is a very simple reason for this: by nature every human being is interested first and foremost in himself or herself. Think about it. Under normal circumstances, wouldn't you rather talk about yourself, your family, your interests, and your accomplishments than listen to someone else talk about theirs? Sin has made us self-centered, so we have to deliberately plan to go against our natural inclination. That is why making a friend and being a friend are so challenging: we have to work at it.

> We should never talk about ourselves, but rather, get others to talk about themselves.

Jesus used this very method to build relationships. Over and over, wherever He went, He never began by talking about Himself. When people in need came to Him, He asked, "What do you want Me to do for you?" He gave them His full attention, asked them a question, listened to their reply, and responded accordingly. Hurting and needy people flocked to Him by the thousands because they knew that He was a man Who cared about them and was interested in them personally. Who would not respond that way? True selflessness is rare in the world, but it should be commonplace among the people of God.

One of the best ways that we can begin building a friendship is by asking questions that focus on the other person's interests. Most people like to talk about themselves, and this is a good way to help them feel comfortable and to gain their trust. These questions can be grouped into four basic areas: family, education, interests, and spiritual things.

The first level of friendship-building questions has to do with family. Why ask people about their family? Because nothing is more dear to them. Here are a few examples. "What are your parents' names? What do they do for a living? How many brothers and sisters do you have? Are you married or single? Do you have any children? What are their names? Where did you grow up? What can you tell me about your family heritage?" The object is to get the other person talking, so avoid deeply personal and probing questions, as well as questions that can be answered with a simple "yes" or "no."

Education is another subject for good conversation. Since virtually everyone has completed at least a certain level of education, everyone has something to talk about. Even a dropout could talk about the failure of the educational system. Knowing where your new friend stands educationally may be very helpful as you seek to help him or her move toward their personal goals, which is part of what friendship is all about. Ask such things as: "How far along are you in school? What school do you attend? Did you drop out of school? If so, why? What are your future educational goals? Do you want to go to college?"

In the third area, ask questions that will get them talking about their personal interests. This is an excellent way to discover what you may have in common. "Do you like sports? What sports are you involved in? Who's your favorite team? Do you have any hobbies? What kind of music do you like? Do you sing or play an instrument? What clubs do you belong to? Do you like to travel? What is your favorite vacation spot?"

The fourth area of friendship-building questions relates to spiritual matters. We should always take a genuine interest in people for who they are, but at the same time have the desire and prayer in our hearts to gauge where they stand in relation to Christ and, as their friend, to lead them to knowledge of Him. In recent years there has been a great upswing of interest in spiritual things in general, particularly in Western culture. More and more people are becoming open to spiritual or supernatural realities. In seeking new friendships, we can get people talking about spiritual matters. "When you attend worship, where do you attend? Do you believe in life after death? Are you a member of a church? Which one? How often do you attend? Are you sure that you will go to Heaven when you die?" People have spiritual interests and questions about life, and we need to be sensitive to them.

Ultimately, our purpose in being a friend should be to encourage, lift up, and help build the character of those with whom we are friends, and to do all we can to assist them in achieving their dreams. Naturally, we cannot do this with everyone we meet, or with anyone right off the bat. Friendship develops in stages. Basically, there are four levels of friendship, and at any given time most of us will have at least one person we know at each level.

ACQUAINTANCE

The lowest level of friendship is that of acquaintance. I believe that everyone in the Body of Christ should have as many people as possible in this category. To the greatest degree practical, we should take the initiative to at least get acquainted with everyone we meet. A friendship of acquaintance is based on occasional contact with very basic and general knowledge of each other. With an acquaintance you talk about the weather, the kids, how your favorite teams did, how school is going, how work is going— general topics that won't cause the person to feel threatened or that you are trying to pry.

Each level of friendship carries certain responsibilities, and at the acquaintance level it is the responsibility to view our acquaintances as divine appointments. As believers, we need to realize that none of our encounters are accidental. God places people in our paths—and us in theirs—that we might be a blessing to each other. He has foreordained that we meet. No one is unimportant or beneath us. Everyone is significant and worthy of our appreciation. We should be alert to discern the reasons God brought them our way. It may be the beginning of a wonderful lifelong friendship.

> God places people in our paths—and us in theirs—that we might be a blessing to each other.

How can good acquaintances be friends? There are several things we can do. First, be alert to every new person around us. Pay attention to their expressions, gestures, and what they are doing. Learn as much about them as possible simply by watching (but not staring).

Second, be careful to wear a cheerful, friendly countenance. In other words, smile at people and be friendly. Some people go around all the time with such scowls or frowns on their faces that no one even wants to be around them, much less talk to them. We should be cheerful and ready to talk, behaving in a manner that encourages others to talk to us.

Next, we should be careful to learn and remember their names. It has been said that the sweetest sound in a person's ear is the sound of his or her own name. People appreciate being remembered as an individual rather than being marked off as a number or just another faceless member of the crowd.

Number four grows naturally from number three: greet them by name the next time we see them. There is no faster way to begin developing a bond of friendship with someone than for that person to realize that we care enough to remember his or her name beyond our first meeting.

A fifth step is to ask questions about their interests. Find out what motivates them—what gets them up in the morning.

Sixth, we should be good listeners.

Seventh, we should remind ourselves of the interest that God has in them, and desire to have that same interest as well.

CASUAL FRIENDSHIP

The next level above acquaintance is casual friendship. Relationships at this level are based on common interests, activities, and concerns. Casual friends meet more frequently than do acquaintances, and in avenues that are more personal: playing tennis or racquetball, quilting or sewing, bird watching, studying astronomy, going to clubs or participating in common hobbies.

One characteristic of casual friendship is the freedom to ask specific questions concerning personal opinions, wishes, dreams, and goals. At this level, the friendship is more involved and more personal than at the acquaintance level. Casual friends enjoy getting together occasionally to talk about or share their common interests. They begin to praise and encourage each other in their achievements and accomplishments. Their attraction is more toward their common interests than toward each other in any emotional sense. Casual friends are not "serious" about each other emotionally. Their friendship is nourished by the pleasure they derive from shared interests.

A casual friendship is one in which the people involved discover they have some things in common that draw them closer, and is the natural outgrowth of an acquaintance relationship. How do we strengthen our relationships with our casual friends? There are several ways.

First, we should seek to discover their strong points. We all have strengths and weaknesses, but too often all we hear about are our weaknesses. It is easy to criticize, but for some reason, we find it much harder to praise and affirm. By focusing on our friends' strengths, we can build them up and help them grow stronger.

Second, we should try to learn about their hopes and desires in life. What are their dreams? If they could have anything in the world, what would it be? If they could do anything they desired, what would they choose? Getting them to talk about their dreams helps them keep those dreams alive and encourages them to pursue them.

A third way to be a good casual friend is to show interest and concern if our friends share a problem with us. We may or may not be able to do much to help, but sometimes what a person needs more than anything else is just a sympathetic listening ear.

Fourth, we need to be honest about ourselves and acknowledge our own faults to our friends when appropriate. We need to be quick to apologize and seek forgiveness if we hurt or offend, and be transparent about our motives. Our honesty will encourage our friends to be honest with us. Honesty promotes honesty and *always* serves the greater good of everyone.

Along with honesty goes trustworthiness. Our friends need to know that they can trust us with information or with confidences they may need to share with us. A good friend does not go around spreading gossip or talking to others about personal matters that another friend shared in confidence.

Finally, as a good friend, we will talk to God about our friends' needs, dreams, and desires. In other words, we will pray for our friends. Although this comes last in the list, praying for our friends is really the most important and significant thing we can do for them.

> Praying for our friends is the most important and significant thing we can do for them.

CLOSE FRIENDSHIP AND FELLOWSHIP

A casual friendship frequently progresses to the next level of close friendship and fellowship. Close friendship is based on mutual life goals and friends at this level enjoy the freedom to suggest mutual projects toward reaching those goals. Most people never get this far in their relationships. So many jump straight from acquaintance to "intimate" because that is the model held up by society, and because they do not know how to go through the friendship-building process. What so many people call "intimate" relationships are not intimate at all, because the people involved have never learned what true intimacy is or how to build toward it. Ultimately, true intimacy has very little to do with sexual relations.

Another characteristic of close friendship is that it is the first relationship that involves genuine common fellowship. Fellowship implies mutual interests and life goals because friends are "fellows" who are in the same "ship" together and therefore traveling the same direction. We can have fellowship only with people who are headed in the same direction as we are. As believers, we can have an acquaintance or even a casual relationship with a Mormon, Buddhist or Hindu, but we can't really have fellowship with them because they are headed in a different direction. Their beliefs and values are different, their life goals are different, and their final destination is different.

Close friends pursue mutual goals and most often share similar values, ideals, and worldviews. It is at this level where unmarried friends begin seriously looking at each other as potential mates: "Are his dreams and goals compatible with mine?" "Is she a person I could share the rest of my life with?" If they are not suited for each other as far as marriage is concerned, this is the time to find out rather than later, after binding and lasting commitments have been made.

One characteristic of this deeper level of friendship and fellowship is the freedom to suggest mutual projects toward reaching life's goals. This means that each friend becomes directly involved in helping the other succeed. Either through advice, referring them to a source that can help, or by giving them personal, financial, or material assistance, close friends take more than just casual interest in their friends' welfare; they get involved.

In our desire to build close friendships we should, first of all, look for and recognize the potential for great achievement in our friends' lives. Once we see them not just for who they are but also for who they can be, we are better prepared to help them fulfill their potential.

Second, we should discover and discuss their specific life goals with them. Without goals, none of us ever go anywhere because we have no road map for our lives and nothing to shoot for. Discussing life goals with a friend is personally enriching and rewarding for both and helps set the stage for making specific plans to reach those goals.

As close friends, we will also assume a measure of personal responsibility for the development of our friends' goals. At this level, we have moved beyond, "I hope you make it," to "I'm going to help you make it."

A fourth step is to help our friends identify and overcome hindrances to the achievement of their goals. Are there financial obstacles? Is further education required? Sometimes people lack the confidence that they can actually reach for their dreams successfully. They may need help overcoming a negative mindset and self-defeating thought patterns.

After identifying potential or actual hindrances, the next step is to help our friends design projects that will move them tangibly and measurably toward their goals. Suppose a wife wants to go back to school to get her degree. If her husband is the friend he should be, he will do everything he can to help her succeed.

It may mean taking on more of the household work to give her time to study, or watching the children alone one or two evenings while she is in class. Close friends are committed to their friends' success.

> Close friends are committed to their friends' success.

A sixth way to be a good close friend is to look for ways to enhance, encourage, and build up our friends' continuing interest in the project. When we get bogged down, it is easy to become discouraged. Knowing there is someone nearby who believes in us can be a real shot in the arm. Perhaps a friend is studying music or learning to play an instrument. One way to encourage him or her would be with a gift: "When I was traveling last weekend, I saw this music and thought of you." Being a continuing source of encouragement for our friends will help them succeed.

Another helpful step would be to share Scriptures we have found that will encourage, strengthen, guide, and help mature our friends.

INTIMATE FRIENDSHIP AND FELLOWSHIP

The fourth and highest level of friendship is that of intimate friendship and fellowship, where friends are committed to the development of each other's character. It is here where true intimacy begins to take place—intimacy of spirit and mind rather than body—a "connectedness" in which friends not only work together on shared interests, but walk together in oneness of spirit. Such intimacy among friends requires the freedom to correct each other, which is why this level is so risky. Being open to correction means making ourselves vulnerable, and many people are not willing to do that. Consequently, they never experience true, intimate friendship with anyone.

Just as with close friends, but to an even greater degree, intimate friends share the same vision, the same life goals, and are walking in the same direction. They are "fellows" on the same "ship." By this understanding, a believer cannot truly be intimate friends with a non-believer because they are not headed in the same direction. The best place to meet and make an intimate friend is on the road to the Kingdom of God.

> The best place to meet and make an intimate friend is on the road to the Kingdom of God.

During His earthly ministry, Jesus had friendships at every level. He had many acquaintances that knew Him by sight, but had little other contact. Casual friends were fewer in number. These were the people who followed Jesus or attached themselves to His ministry in some way but were not close enough to know His heart. Jesus' close friends included the 12 men He chose as His disciples, as well as a few others outside that circle, such as Mary, Martha, Lazarus, and several women who often accompanied Jesus and supported Him out of their means. Of the 12 disciples, three—Peter, James, and John—were favored to become Jesus' intimate friends.

Those three alone accompanied Jesus to the Mount of Transfiguration. They alone went with Him into the room where Jairus' daughter lay dead and witnessed Jesus bring her back to life. Peter, James, and John truly were Jesus' companions. A companion is one with whom you explore the deep thoughts of your heart, your dreams, aspirations, fears, weaknesses, and desires.

There were things that Jesus told the disciples that He did not tell anyone else. Many were the times when Jesus taught the multitudes in parables and later, privately, explained them in greater detail to His disciples. Jesus' casual friends were interested in His interests, His close friends were committed to His goals, but His intimate friends were after His heart.

The presence or absence of commitment is the main way to distinguish between levels of friendship. Acquaintances and casual friendships carry little or no commitment and the ebb and flow of life constantly takes some of them out of our sphere of influence and brings others into it. Close and intimate friendships are committed to the long-term.

Intimate friends are committed to the development of each other's character. That means that they are driven to do everything in their power to help each other be better than the day before. We need to ask ourselves, "Do I have that kind of friend?" but even more importantly, "Am I that kind of friend?"

True and intimate friends look out for each other's welfare. They are not afraid to say, "Don't do that, because it's not good for you." They will not say or do anything or put pressure on each other that could lead to damaged or compromised character. If, for example, your so-called dating "friend" is always pressuring you to have sex, you need to reevaluate the nature of that friendship. A true friend will not put that kind of pressure on you. Anyone who does should be relegated to a casual friend or an acquaintance. Save your intimate friendship for someone who will be committed to your character.

> True and intimate friends look out for each other's welfare.

As believers, we should reserve our intimate friendships for other believers, because then we are mutually committed to helping each other live and walk in the will and purpose of God and to develop godly character. This does not mean that we should not cultivate friendly relationships with non-believers. How else can we influence them for Christ? It does mean that we should remember that no matter how much we may have in common with our non-believing friends in the areas of interests, hobbies, and the like, we are on completely different planes spiritually. Our intimate friends should be people who are seeking the Kingdom of God just as we are.

One characteristic of true intimacy is the capacity to both give and receive correction with grace and appreciation. Intimate friends love each other enough not to let sin, errors, or wrong direction go uncorrected. They respect and trust each other enough to receive correction without resentment or suspicion. Intimate friends are comfortable in the knowledge that they are committed to each other's welfare and greatest good.

Intimate friendship carries with it the mutual responsibility of open honesty with discretion. Openness is essential to intimacy, but true friends will carefully guard each other's confidences. There are some things we can tell our dearest friends that no one else needs to know.

Here are some practical steps we can take to become good intimate friends. First, be ready, willing, and available to give our friends comfort and support during their times of trial and sorrow. At the same time, we should be just as ready to rejoice with them in times of success and prosperity. It has been said that shared sorrow is halved while shared joy is doubled. Friends support each other in joy or sorrow, in good times or bad.

Second, we should assume a measure of personal responsibility for our friends' reputations. We should be jealous for the integrity of their good name and quick to defend them from criticism or attack. If criticism and correction are justifiable, we should do it privately and in a manner that preserves our friends' dignity and honor.

Third, we need to be sensitive to traits and attitudes that need improvement, not only in our friends' lives, but also in our own. If we are committed to personal character development, we must be open to ways to improve and help our friends in the same way.

Similarly, we must discern the basic causes of character deficiencies in our friends as well as in ourselves. Seeking character flaws in our friends is not for the purpose of criticism, but for correction. We want them to become the best people they can be. As concerned outsiders, we can see their character flaws better than they can. This is a two-way street, however. Our friends can also see in us character deficiencies that we cannot see in ourselves. True friends are committed to working with each other to become better people.

A fifth step is to build our friends' interest in correcting their own deficiencies by asking them to tell us about ours. This goes hand in hand with number four.

Sixth, we should search the Scriptures for keys to building strong character, either alone or with our friends, and discuss our findings. In this way we can grow together.

Finally, no matter what, we should always be committed to faithfulness, loyalty, and availability.

DISTINGUISHING QUALITIES OF FRIENDSHIP

Friendship is not a gift, but is the result of hard work. Christlike character is not built overnight. It comes only through committed effort. Friends working together to achieve these common goals will find success easier than those who try to do it alone. Mutual encouragement and accountability make a big difference in how quickly we progress toward our goal.

> Friendship is not a gift, but is the result of hard work.

With this in mind, we need to consider what kind of qualities we should look for in a friend, and then endeavor to build those in ourselves so that we too can be good friends.

- *Truthfulness versus deception.* Are we truthful and honest in all our dealings? Is there any deceptiveness in our speech or manner?

- *Obedience versus willfulness.* Are we obedient to what we ought to do, rather than willfully doing only what we want to do or what we feel we can get away with?

- *Sincerity versus hypocrisy.* Are we sincere in our commitment to God and to our friends? Are we committed to their character, or only to what we can get from them? Are we hypocritical, hiding an ulterior motive under a guise of love?

- *Virtue versus defilement.* Are we committed to keeping ourselves clean and pure in mind and body? Do we act from the highest motives and most honorable intentions?

- *Boldness versus fearfulness.* Are we secure with who we are in Christ? Are we confident in standing up for what is right, even if it means standing alone?

- *Forgiveness versus rejection.* Do we have a forgiving spirit, ready to be reconciled with someone who has offended us? Are we humble enough to seek forgiveness when we have offended?

- *Joyfulness versus withdrawal.* Do we approach life from a fundamental position of joy? Have we discovered that joy is a quality and fruit of the Holy Spirit and therefore not dependent upon our circumstances?

- *Flexibility versus resistance.* Are we willing to allow others to be different and to make mistakes? Are we adaptable, or do we resist change?

- *Availability versus dominance.* Are we available and willing to help without forcing our advice and assistance on others? Are we willing to listen and consider other viewpoints, or do we always insist on our own way?

- *Endurance versus giving up.* Are we patient? Do we possess the presence of mind and strength of spirit to persevere through trial or hardship? Do we have "staying power"?

- *Reverence versus disrespect.* Are we reverent toward God in all things? Are we respectful toward other people in every circumstance?

- *Diligence versus slothfulness.* Are we diligent in our work and in the pursuit of our goals, or are we lazy, content with doing just enough to get by?

- *Security versus anxiety.* Are we secure in our own personality and identity? Are we complete within ourselves or do we look to others to supply our lack? Are we anxious or fearful about life or about what others may think of us?

- *Wisdom versus natural inclinations.* Do we think before we act? Are we guided by sound principles and values, or do we simply flow with the tide, acting on impulse?

- *Discernment versus imperceptiveness.* Are we sensitive to the Spirit of God and to the environment around us? Do we pick up on the moods and feelings of others?

- *Faith versus presumption.* Does our faith in Christ guide our actions and decisions, or do we act on impulse or the whim of the moment?

- *Discretion versus simple-mindedness.* Do we think before we speak or act, or do we "shoot from the hip"? Do we consider beforehand the possible consequences of our words or actions?

- *Self-control versus self-gratification.* Do we exercise appropriate restraint in speech, behavior, and desire, or simply act according to what feels good? Are we guided by discipline and modesty or driven by greed, lust, ego, or hormones?

- *Thriftiness versus extravagance.* Are we careful with money or does it slip through our fingers as fast as we make it? Are we frugal without being stingy and generous without being reckless?

- *Creativity versus underachievement.* Are we self-motivated and self-starting, or do we need someone to always direct us in what to do and how to do it? Are we innovators, always looking for new ideas, or do we simply follow routine?

- *Enthusiasm versus negativity.* Is life perennially fresh and exciting for us and full of opportunity, or are we always nay-saying other people's thoughts, dreams, and creative ideas? Are we optimistic about the future, or always down about life?

- *Resourcefulness versus wastefulness.* Do we use our time, material, and energy constructively and efficiently? Do we value quality? Can we distinguish between the important and the unimportant, and between the good and the best?

- *Punctuality versus tardiness.* Do we value other people's time or are we consistently late? Do we organize and plan ahead to be punctual? Can other people depend on us to be timely in our commitments?

- *Contentment versus covetousness.* Are we content with what we have or driven by the craving for more? Are our needs simple, or are we hard to satisfy? Are we willing to let go of some things in order to hold on to the most important things?

- *Gratefulness versus pride.* Do we have an "attitude of gratitude" toward God and toward other people? Do we appreciate what others do for us or are we too proud to acknowledge how much we need them?

- *Neatness versus disorganization.* Are we orderly in our habits and behavior or do we tend to let things go? Do we respect others' "space"? Do we stay on top of bills, commitments, and other obligations, or do we neglect them?

- *Initiative versus unresponsiveness.* Do we look for something to do or wait until someone directs us? Do we seek to exceed expectations and our own past performance, or do only the bare minimum that is required?

- *Courage versus cowardice.* Do we stand behind our convictions? Do we stand behind our friends and family? Do we stand behind our word or cave in under opposition?

- *Responsibility versus irresponsibility.* Are we reliable? Can others depend on us to do what we said we would do? Are we willing to be held accountable for our actions and our words?

- *Decisiveness versus double-mindedness.* Can we make decisions and stand behind them, or are we always second-guessing ourselves? Do we accept our responsibility or do we defer to others decisions that are rightfully ours to make?

- *Loyalty versus unfaithfulness.* Are we true to our commitments? Do our friends have the confidence that we will always be there for them or have we let them down too many times?

- *Attentiveness versus inapproachability.* Are we good listeners? Do we pay attention when others speak to us? Do they come to us with a fear, a burden, or a joy, or do we appear cold and aloof, with an air that says, "Leave me alone"?

- *Sensitivity versus carelessness.* Are we watchful of others' feelings and moods and of how our words and actions may affect them? Does our body language show that we care about them and are genuinely interested in them?

- *Fairness versus partiality.* Are we willing to listen to both sides of a story? Do we seek truth, justice, and equity in every situation or do we display bias and prejudice and constantly play favorites?

- *Compassion versus indifference.* Are we moved to action by the pain, suffering, or need of others, or are we too caught up with our own affairs to bother with them?

- *Gentleness versus harshness.* Are we mature enough to speak softly, even in rebuke, knowing that "a gentle answer turns away wrath, but a harsh word stirs up anger" (Prov. 15:1)?

- *Deference versus rudeness.* Do we defer rebuke or correction to a private setting, or do we inflict hurt, humiliation, and resentment by scolding in public and endangering our relationship?

- *Meekness versus anger.* Are we meek toward others, exhibiting "strength under control," or do we lash out in anger or violence, displaying a lack of self-control, which is weakness? Do we desire to bless people rather than hurt them?

I personalized these distinguishing characteristics of friendship by describing them in the first person plural in order to remind us that the initiative should always be ours. Once we understand the principles, we are responsible for applying them. The best way to *make* a friend is by *being* a friend. True friendship, like true love, always focuses on the other instead of the self.

The best way to make a friend is by being a friend.

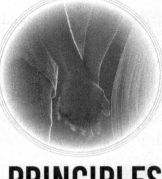

PRINCIPLES

1. True friendship is based on love, which comes from God.

2. Focusing on the other person is one of the steadfast principles of friendship.

3. A friendship of acquaintance is based on occasional contact with a very basic and general knowledge of each other.

4. We should view our acquaintances as divine appointments.

5. Casual friendship is based on common interests, activities, and concerns.

6. A casual friendship is nourished by the pleasure derived from shared interests.

7. Close friendship is based on mutual life goals with the freedom to suggest mutual projects toward reaching those goals.

8. Intimate friends are committed to the development of each other's character.

9. Intimate friends have the freedom to correct each other.

10. Intimate friends share the same vision and life goals, and are walking in the same direction.

11. Intimate friendship carries with it the mutual responsibility of open honesty with discretion.

12. True friendship, like true love, focuses on the other instead of the self.

CHAPTER THREE

MYTHS OF MATE-FINDING

THROUGH MY MANY YEARS OF PRE-MARITAL AND MARRIAGE counseling, I have discovered that one of the main causes of problems after marriage is the lack of knowledge or inaccurate knowledge before marriage. It never ceases to amaze me how many misconceptions, self-delusions, erroneous assumptions, and naive "pie-in-the-sky" expectations people bring into a marriage relationship. Bad information spawns unrealistic expectations, which lead inevitably to disappointment and disillusionment later. As computer programmers like to say, "Garbage in, garbage out."

A successful dating life, not to mention a successful marriage afterward, depends on accurate knowledge. Knowledge is the curative for bad information. Proverbs 24:3-4 says, "By wisdom a house is built, and through understanding it is established; through knowledge its rooms are filled with rare and beautiful treasures." Wisdom, understanding, and knowledge can be found in many different ways, but the two best sources are God Himself and the wise counsel of trusted mentors. Again, the words of Proverbs: "The fear of the Lord is the beginning of knowledge, but fools despise wisdom and discipline" (Prov. 1:7), and, "Plans fail for lack of counsel, but with many advisers they succeed" (Prov. 15:22).

> Knowledge is the curative for bad information.

Success rarely occurs without planning, and plans without wisdom usually fail. God has given us the capacity to make plans, but He expects us to look to Him to make them succeed: "In his heart a man plans his course, but the Lord determines his steps" (Prov. 16:9).

From this we find two principles that are necessary for our success in anything. First, we need a plan, and second, we need godly wisdom for executing that plan successfully. The plan is our responsibility; the wisdom for its execution comes from God. If we want a successful dating life, we must plan for that success. Unless we plan for success, it won't happen. Then we must learn and follow God's principles in order for our plan to succeed. We must make plans in our hearts and then trust the Lord to guide our steps.

Even careful, well-laid plans will fail if they are based on faulty information. That is why it is important to have accurate knowledge before we start. It is much easier to avoid mistakes in the beginning than to correct them in midstream.

Bearing this in mind, it is time to do a little myth smashing. A myth is an idea or a concept that is widely held to be true, yet has no foundation for its veracity—its supposed truth has never been tested. It is an unfounded or false notion that many people nonetheless assume to be true. There are many myths in our culture regarding the finding of a mate that continue to flourish, even though they are the cause of much confusion and disappointment for people who get caught up in them. I want to take a close look at two of them.

MYTH NUMBER ONE: GOD HAS ONE SPECIAL PERSON FOR ME

One popular idea is that God has for each of us one special, ideal person and that we need to wait until that person crosses our path. At that time lights will flash, bells will ring, our knees will go weak, and our whole life will suddenly be wrapped up in that person. Many of us have been taught in the Church that God has a specific person for us—a "Prince Charming" for every woman and a "Sleeping Beauty" for every man—and only that specific person will do. We have been told that we need to pray and fast and search until that specific person appears. The assumption of many is, "If God made me, then surely He made some special someone somewhere who is perfectly suited for me."

This is a myth. There are no Scriptural grounds to support the idea that there is one and only one "Mr. Right" or "Miss Ideal" for every person. Let's be honest. There are six billion people in the world. If there is only one person in six billion who is right for you, what is the likelihood that the two of you will meet up?

In reality, there are thousands, perhaps millions of people in the world who are potential mates for you because of similarities in personality, character, values, and interests to your own. Even if you find the "perfect" person and marry him or her, you are almost certain to meet others along the way who would also have been "perfect" for you. In some cases, they may even appear to be better suited for you than the person you married.

This is one of the problems behind the divorce epidemic in our society. People marry that "perfect" person, expecting life now to be grand and glorious and enchanting, like a fairy tale. Once the new wears off and reality sets in, many couples become dissatisfied because the reality does not live up to their expectations. In the midst of their discontentment, one or both of them may meet someone new who seems to be just what they have been looking for. An affair begins, a divorce follows, and off they go looking for their fairy tale again.

People who are deceived by this myth get married believing that their "perfect" spouse is the only one for them and that being married to this person will solve all their problems of lust or a wandering eye. If a woman says, "I have found 'Mr. Right,'" she may very well expect that she will no longer be attracted to any other men or tempted by their appeal. A man who says, "I have found the perfect woman for me" may feel that his eye could never be drawn to another woman.

This expectation can cause a particular problem for believers. A husband is enjoying married life when all of a sudden, during a business trip, he meets another woman who attracts him in much the same way his wife does. Then it happens again somewhere else on vacation. Before long he begins to feel guilty, as if he is being unfaithful to his wife simply because he is attracted to other women. He feels dirty and sinful, thinking, "I'm married. I love my wife. I'm not supposed to feel this way." At this point, one of two things may happen. He may become so guilt-ridden that he surrenders in defeat and enters into an affair, or he may withdraw and become unsociable out of fear that he cannot trust himself.

Many married believers experience guilt over feeling attracted to people other than their mates. This sense of guilt is often due, at least in part, to this erroneous idea that there is one and only one "right" person for them to marry. In reality, there are any number of people who would be suitable. A difference in timing or circumstances could have resulted in their marrying someone else.

Marrying one "suitable" person does not mean all the others vanish away. No matter how much we may love our mate, no matter how devoted we are to him or her, we will always meet others of the opposite sex who attract us. That is natural, normal, and inevitable. How we deal with that reality will, in large measure, determine whether we experience success or failure. That is why accurate knowledge is so important. Once we know that there are many "suitable" people we could marry, and not just one, we will not be so surprised by the attraction we feel toward some.

Smashing this myth leads to two important conclusions. First, if there are any number of "suitable" candidates for us to marry, then marrying one out of that number becomes a *choice* that we make. Second, the choice that we make to marry a particular person calls for a firm *commitment* on our part to be faithful to the one we choose. *Choice* and *commitment* go hand in hand.

MYTH NUMBER TWO: GOD CHOOSES THE PERSON HE WANTS ME TO MARRY

A second common myth about marriage is the idea that God chooses the person He wants you to marry. This myth is a natural outgrowth of the first one. After all, if God has created one and only one special person for each of us, then obviously He has chosen that person for us and vice versa. We have already seen that the idea of there being one special person for us is false. The idea that God chooses our mates for us is just as false.

Some folks have the idea—and some have even been taught in their churches—that the Lord somehow will reveal to them who they are to marry. It may be in a dream, or through a prophecy, or some other mystical or supernatural means. Some even imagine that they can sit on the edge of their bed, close their eyes, open their Bible, and put their finger randomly on a page, so that when they open their eyes they will see the name of their future spouse. If a woman sees the name Joshua, for example, she will start looking expectantly for a guy named Joshua to come into her life. On the surface, this sounds like a nice, "spiritual" approach. It has some problems, however. What if her finger lands on the name "Elimelech," or "Zerubbabel"? What are the chances of her finding a man carrying one of those names?

Even in the Church there are a lot of people doing some really spooky stuff in an attempt to find a spouse. Too many times I have heard someone say something like, "Last night while I was praying, I had a vision where the Lord told me that I am going to marry 'John.'" Wherever that vision came from, it did not come from the Lord, and here's why. If God told this woman in a vision that she is supposed to marry John, then God has violated both her will and John's. By *telling* her she is to marry John, God has *violated* her will to choose John, as well as John's will to *refuse*. God created all of us with the freedom to choose, and He never violates that freedom.

I remember one situation where a young woman came to me and said, "Brother Myles, I had a dream and the Lord told me I am supposed to marry so-and-so. I know it's true. I went and got confirmation from a few brothers and sisters, and they all said, 'Yes, he's the one.'" She even had Scripture to back it up: "He who finds a wife finds what is good and receives favor from the Lord" (Prov. 18:22).

After she finished sharing this with me, I simply asked, "Have you checked with him?"

"No," she answered, "I'm waiting for the Lord to tell him."

"In that case," I said, "don't count on marrying him. This is not from God. If it were, He would have given this young man the same message He gave you."

She got angry with me because I did not agree with her prophecy, and left. Three or four months passed with nothing else happening, and then the man she was so certain about started going with someone else. She came back to my office and started crying. Through her tears she said, "Brother Myles, he doesn't seem to be listening to the Holy Spirit."

I tried to help her understand. "If you believe that God chose him for you, then by his refusal to choose you, you are making

God out to be a liar. God is *not* a liar. Secondly, you are making God out to be the cause of your broken heart. God is not a breaker of hearts, but a mender of hearts. Third, by insisting that God is the one who chooses your mate, you are making Him responsible for the success or failure of your relationship."

God does not choose our mate. Nowhere does the Bible present God as choosing mates for His people; the choice is always ours. This is a principle God laid down from the very beginning. In Genesis 1:27 we read, "So God created man in His own image, in the image of God He created him; male and female He created them." What are the characteristics of God that make Him God? We could name millions, but three are particularly significant here: God is Creator, God is all-knowing, and God has a will.

> God does not choose your mate... the choice is always yours.

God created man in His own image. He created us not as robots but as free-thinking, free-acting individuals. Robots are capable only of responding to their programming; they cannot truly think for themselves or initiate any independent actions. Robots are incapable of love. God is a Lover by nature, Who desires creatures who would love Him in return. For that to be possible, He had to create us with the capacity to choose—or to reject—His love.

As free-thinking, free-acting individuals, we are like the God who created us. We have the ability to create, not out of nothing as God did, but within the sphere of our dominion. We can take what is around us and improve it and fashion new things out of the raw elements. We also have the ability to learn and to keep on learning. Finally, we have a will, which we can exercise freely.

When God created man, He began with the male, Adam, and created Eve, the female, later. Even then, God did not *choose* Eve to be Adam's mate. Adam made that choice himself. This is clear through a careful reading of the second chapter of Genesis.

> *The Lord God said, "It is not good for the man to be alone. I will make a helper suitable for him." ... So the Lord God caused the man to fall into a deep sleep; and while he was sleeping, He took one of the man's ribs and closed up the place with flesh. Then the Lord God made a woman from the rib He had taken out of the man, and He brought her to the man. The man said, "This is now bone of my bones and flesh of my flesh; she shall be called 'woman,' for she was taken out of man." For this reason a man will leave his father and mother and be united to his wife, and they will become one flesh* (Gen. 2:18, 21-24).

God neither chose the woman for the man, nor gave her to him. God brought her to the man and he accepted her. Adam chose Eve. Nothing else is suggested or implied. As a matter of fact, in the original Hebrew, the word translated *brought* literally means "put on display." God displayed the woman He had made and presented her to Adam, who accepted what God presented to him.

Whether God chose and gave Eve to Adam or whether Adam chose her may seem to be a minor point, but in reality, it is very important. Adam, like every human being since, was responsible for his own choices. Whenever he made poor choices, he could not turn around and blame God for the consequences of those choices. That didn't stop him from trying, however. After he and Eve disobeyed God by eating of the fruit of the forbidden tree, God confronted them with their sin. He asked Adam, "Have you eaten from the tree that I commanded you not to eat from?" (Gen. 3:11b) Adam answered, "The woman You put here with me—she gave me some fruit from the tree, and I ate it" (Gen. 3:12). All of a sudden, at least in Adam's mind, God is responsible for the disaster because He gave the woman to Adam, and she prompted him to eat the forbidden fruit. Try as he would, however, Adam could not evade being responsible for his own choices.

What this means for us is, like Adam and Eve, we are free to choose and therefore bear responsibility for our choices and their consequences. This is just as true in our relationships as anywhere else. God may bring a potential mate across our path, but He does not choose that person for us. We make that choice ourselves, based on what we learn about that person and on the nature of the friendship that develops. It is certainly appropriate to ask God for *wisdom* in making our choice about a mate, but He will not choose for us. The choice is still ours.

ISAAC AND REBEKAH

The Bible contains many examples of this principle at work. One of the best, perhaps, is the Old Testament story of how Abraham's son, Isaac, found his wife, Rebekah. In those days, it was customary for a father to take responsibility for finding a wife for his son. Arranged marriages were quite common in that culture. One day Abraham, wanting to ensure the best for Isaac, dispatched a servant to go to his ancestral homeland and find a wife for his son.

> *Abraham was now old and well advanced in years, and the Lord had blessed him in every way. He said to the chief servant in his household, the one in charge of all that he had, "Put your hand under my thigh. I want you to swear by the Lord, the God of heaven and the God of earth, that you will not get a wife for my son from the daughters of the Canaanites, among whom I am living, but will go to my country and my own relatives and get a wife for my son Isaac." The servant asked him, "What if the woman is unwilling to come back with me to this land? Shall I then take your son back to the country you came from?" "Make sure that you do not take my son back there," Abraham said. "The Lord, the God of heaven, who brought me out of my father's household and my native land and who spoke to me and promised me on oath, saying, 'To your offspring I will give this land'—he will send his angel before you so that you can get a wife for my son from there. If the woman is unwilling to come back with you, then you will be released from this oath of mine. Only do not take my son back there." So the servant put his hand under the thigh of his master Abraham and swore an oath to him concerning this matter (Gen. 24:1-9).*

Several things are important to note here. First, Abraham sent his servant to get a wife for Isaac from Abraham's own kinfolk. Beyond that restriction, Abraham was not specific. Abraham did not choose a specific person for Isaac; he merely limited the field of choice. Second, the conversation between Abraham and his servant make it clear that they both recognized the possibility that the woman the servant found, whoever she was, might *choose* not to come with him. Nothing was mandated beforehand; nothing was set in stone. Third, Abraham assured his servant that an angel of God would go before him and help make his mission a success. An angel is a *guide*, not a dictator. He could lead the servant in the right direction, but he could not—would not—make the choice himself.

In obedience to Abraham's wishes, the servant took ten camels and many good gifts with him and set out on his long journey. Upon arriving in the town of Nahor in Abraham's homeland, the servant stopped beside the town's well.

Then he prayed, "O Lord, God of my master Abraham, give me success today, and show kindness to my master Abraham. See, I am standing beside this spring, and the daughters of the townspeople are coming out to draw water. May it be that when I say to a girl, 'Please let down your jar that I may have a drink,' and she says, 'Drink, and I'll water your camels too'—let her be the one you have chosen for your servant Isaac. By this I will know that you have shown kindness to my master." Before he had finished praying, Rebekah came out with her jar on her shoulder. She was the daughter of Bethuel son of Milcah, who was the wife of Abraham's brother

Nahor. The girl was very beautiful, a virgin; no man had ever lain with her. She went down to the spring, filled her jar and came up again. The servant hurried to meet her and said, "Please give me a little water from your jar." "Drink, my lord," she said, and quickly lowered the jar to her hands and gave him a drink. After she had given him a drink, she said, "I'll draw water for your camels too, until they have finished drinking" (Gen. 24:12-19).

At this point, the servant makes a very specific request of the Lord. He asks God to show him the very person He has "chosen" to be Isaac's wife. Despite the specific use of the word "chosen" here in reference to God, the context of this entire story indicates that, while God is actively involved in guiding the process of finding a wife for Isaac, it is the people involved who actually make the choices. God answered the servant's prayer and brought him directly to Rebekah, granddaughter of Abraham's brother Nahor. Rebekah was Abraham's grandniece and, therefore, Isaac's cousin.

Rebekah's family welcomes Abraham's servant into their house, and he insists on telling them his business even before eating. After relating his tale of his assignment to find a wife for Isaac and his journey to Nahor and how God answered his prayer by bringing him to Rebekah, the servant asks his hosts for a decision.

"Now if you will show kindness and faithfulness to my master, tell me; and if not, tell me, so I may know which way to turn." Laban and Bethuel answered, "This is

from the Lord; we can say nothing to you one way or the other. Here is Rebekah; take her and go, and let her become the wife of your master's son, as the Lord has directed." When Abraham's servant heard what they said, he bowed down to the ground before the Lord. Then the servant brought out gold and silver jewelry and articles of clothing and gave them to Rebekah; he also gave costly gifts to her brother and to her mother. Then he and the men who were with him ate and drank and spent the night there. When they got up the next morning, he said, "Send me on my way to my master." But her brother and her mother replied, "Let the girl remain with us ten days or so; then you may go." But he said to them, "Do not detain me, now that the Lord has granted success to my journey. Send me on my way so I may go to my master." Then they said, "Let's call the girl and ask her about it." So they called Rebekah and asked her, "Will you go with this man?" "I will go," she said. So they sent their sister Rebekah on her way, along with her nurse and Abraham's servant and his men. …So the servant took Rebekah and left.…[Isaac] went out to the field one evening to meditate, and as he looked up, he saw camels approaching. Rebekah also looked up and saw Isaac. She got down from her camel and asked the servant, "Who is that man in the field coming to meet us?" "He is my master," the servant answered. So she took her veil and covered herself. Then the servant told Isaac all he had done. Isaac brought her into the tent of his mother Sarah, and he married Rebekah. So she became his wife, and he loved her; and Isaac was comforted after his mother's death (Gen. 24:49-59,61,63-67).

These verses clearly show that, while the Lord was guiding the process of selecting a wife for Isaac, the *choice* still remained with the human beings involved. First, Rebekah's father, Bethuel, and her brother, Laban, gave their approval and permission for Rebekah to go. This, too, was customary in that ancient culture.

Second, when Abraham's servant was anxious to depart with Rebekah on the return journey, her family called her and asked her directly: "Will you go with this man?" She answered, "Yes." Even though God was guiding the process and, even though the male leaders in Rebekah's family gave their permission, in the end, it was Rebekah herself who made the choice.

Third, after arriving home with Rebekah, Abraham's servant explained everything to Isaac, who then married Rebekah and loved her. While Isaac's choice of Rebekah is not plainly stated, it is clearly implied. No one ordered him to marry Rebekah and there is no indication or suggestion that he was following a command from God to do so. As it was with Adam choosing Eve, Isaac chose Rebekah when she was presented to him.

When it comes to finding a mate, God will give us guidance, wisdom, and direction when we ask for it. He may even bring a suitable person (or persons) across our path. What God will *not* do, however, is choose our mate for us. We must make that decision based on all the information we have. He may guide us, but the final choice is ours.

DON'T JUDGE BY THE WORLD'S STANDARDS

If there is no one single special person for us, and if God does not choose our mate for us, then how do we choose the right mate? What criteria should we use? Unfortunately, many believers take their cue from the standards of society, which is unwise considering our society's generally poor track record regarding marital success. Among the general public, over half of all marriages end in divorce, and in some sectors of the Church, the figure is not much lower. Part of the problem for believers in building strong relationships is that the world's standards provide the only model they know.

Generally speaking, relationships in the world are built according to one or more of four basic criteria: physical appearance, social status, intellectual ability, and financial means. The most important criterion of all, the spiritual dimension, is usually ignored, at least until problems crop up in the relationship. By the time many couples begin paying attention to the spiritual aspects of their relationship, it is often too late.

> By the time many couples begin paying attention to the spiritual aspects of their relationship, it is often too late.

Someone might ask, "What's wrong with the world's standards? Why shouldn't I look for these things in a mate?" In and of themselves, there is nothing wrong with any of these, but by themselves they are not a sound basis upon which to build a strong, long-term relationship. Such a relationship must be built on permanent qualities, and the world's standards are temporary. Any of them can change in an instant.

Many people choose a mate by searching for someone who is "handsome" or "beautiful." What do those words mean? Whose criteria do we use in determining whether or not a prospective candidate is attractive enough physically? Where do our standards of physical beauty come from? *Vogue?* Movie stars? Fashion shows?

The world's standard for physical attractiveness is the beauty of the supermodel, a "standard" attainable by less than one percent of the world's population. What kind of a standard is that? Nevertheless, that is the standard our society promotes. People judge and evaluate their mates and potential mates according to an unattainable standard.

Physical attractiveness only goes so far. If a couple builds their relationship on such a standard, what happens when physical beauty begins to fade? How will she feel when his gorgeous hair turns gray or comes out, or when his trim, athletic abs turn into a potbelly? How will he feel when she starts to fill out in all the "wrong" places and develops a double chin? What if they need dentures? If they want a happy, long-term relationship, they'd better have more going for them than simply physical attraction.

Social status is another false standard for choosing a mate. Many people, particularly women, look to their mate to provide them with upward mobility in society. They want to marry into a "good" family with money, a well-respected name, and an influential position. Like physical appearance, social status can change, often quickly. All it takes is a downturn in the economy or some poor investment choices to knock a couple several rungs down the social ladder.

Some people look for a mate based on intellectual capacity or educational accomplishments. Is she a college graduate? What field is she going into? Is he going to be an engineer? A doctor? A lawyer? A businessman? A corporate executive? Even these considerations are influenced by concerns of money and social status. After all, we often hear someone dream, "I want to marry a doctor," or, "I want to marry a lawyer." How often do we hear someone say, "I want to marry a ditch digger," or, "I want to marry a grocery store clerk"? There is nothing at all wrong with being a ditch digger or a grocery store clerk, but our society has conditioned us to think there is.

Another false standard for choosing a mate is basing the choice on his or her financial means. "Can he support me?" "Can she take care of me?" "Can we live on one income, or will both of us have to work?" While these are legitimate and important questions—persons contemplating marriage need to consider carefully whether or not they are prepared for the financial realities of married life—financial means alone is not the basis for choosing a mate or for getting married.

JUDGE ACCORDING TO GOD'S STANDARDS

Finding a mate is not a matter of meeting up with that one "magic" person or persuading God to cause someone to fall in love with us. The key to finding the right mate is first to identify the qualities and character that we will hold as our standard without compromise, and then evaluate the potential candidates we meet according to those standards. A woman may be beautiful but have poor character. A man may be a business genius, making money left and right, but lack common courtesy, sensitivity, and compassion.

Our primary concern should be not how a person looks or what a person does, but what kind of a person he or she is. Appearances are deceiving. All of us are born with talents and gifts, but character must be developed, carefully cultivated, and nurtured over time. This is one reason why it is important to take time to get to know a person before getting into a serious relationship. Just about anyone you meet can dazzle you for a little while with charm, consideration, and politeness. Stay with him long enough, though, and his character will begin to show through. What you should be alert for is to see whether his outward behavior is a true reflection of his character. Solid character will reflect itself in consistent behavior, while poor character will seek to hide behind deceptive words and actions.

> All of us are born with talents and gifts, but character must be developed, carefully cultivated, and nurtured over time.

When we look into the Word of God, we find that any time God chose people for His purposes, He always looked for character and internal qualities, not physical attributes. Moses was slow of speech and a stutterer, yet God chose him to go before Pharaoh and bring the Israelites out of Egypt. When God set out to deliver His people from the marauding Midianites, he chose Gideon, who described himself as the least in his father's family, of the least of the tribes of Israel. God also told Gideon that He would give victory using only 300 men chosen not by specific name, but by the characteristic way they drank water from the stream. David was the youngest and smallest of Jesse's sons, not considered even significant enough to be brought before Samuel, who was seeking God's man to be king. Nevertheless, David was God's choice because he had a heart for God.

In Acts 6, when servant ministers were needed in the church in Jerusalem, the apostles, under the Holy Spirit's leading, directed the church to "choose seven men from among you who are known to be full of the Spirit and wisdom" (Acts 6:3). The Spirit laid down the qualities; the church chose the men.

A similar situation is found in First Timothy 3, in which Paul gives Timothy guidelines for selecting overseers and deacons for the church.

> *Now the overseer must be above reproach, the husband of but one wife, temperate, self-controlled, respectable, hospitable, able to teach, not given to drunkenness, not violent but gentle, not quarrelsome, not a lover of money. He must manage his own family well and see that his children obey him with proper respect.... He must also have a good reputation with outsiders.... Deacons, likewise, are to be men worthy of respect, sincere, not indulging in much wine, and not pursuing dishonest gain. They must keep hold of the deep truths of the faith with a clear conscience.... A deacon must be the husband of but one wife and must manage his children and his household well* (1 Tim. 3:2-4;7-9,12).

Once again, the focus is on *character* and *qualifications* rather than on identifying specific people by name. Timothy was to make selections according to those qualifications. Anyone whose lifestyle demonstrated the necessary qualities was an acceptable candidate. The qualities of character that Paul laid down here for overseers and deacons sound also like excellent qualities to look for in a mate: "above reproach…temperate, self-controlled, respectable, hospitable…not given to drunkenness, not violent but gentle, not quarrelsome, not a lover of money." These are the kinds of things God looks for in a person He chooses. These are the standards by which He measures, and we should do the same.

In the course of daily living, there may be many people who will cross our paths who demonstrate these qualities. According to these standards, any one of them could be a potential mate. The only way to know for sure is by getting to know them; by building a friendship with them. These kinds of qualities will not come out through a casual acquaintance. We must spend a lot of time with someone in order to discern his or her character. Anyone can put on his best behavior for a while. At some point, however, he will show his true colors. How he responds to the circumstances of life will reveal his character. If we know ahead of time the qualities and character that we are looking for in a mate, it will be much easier for us to recognize that person whenever he or she comes along.

Choosing a life partner is not a matter of getting a magical sense or a supernatural revelation that, "This is the one." It is a matter of getting to know people who cross your path and evaluating them by the uncompromising standards you have established beforehand, recognizing always that you will find more than one person who meets those standards. That is what makes finding a life partner a *choice* in the truest sense of the word. Out of all the people you know, out of all the friendships you develop, out of all the legitimate "possibles" before you, you choose one person with whom you wish to spend the rest of your life. This is not a flighty, haphazard, head-in-the-clouds choice, but a deliberate, sober, feet-firmly-planted-on-the-ground decision. It is reaching the place where you approach another and say with deliberate confidence, "I choose you."

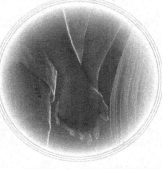

PRINCIPLES

1. God does not have one and only one special person for us.

2. There are any number of people in the world who are potential mates for us because of similarities in personality, character, values, and interests to our own.

3. If there are any number of "suitable" candidates for us to marry, then marrying one of them becomes a choice that we make.

4. The choice that we make to marry a particular person calls for a firm commitment on our part to be faithful to the one we choose.

5. God does not choose the person He wants us to marry.

6. God created all of us with the freedom to choose, and He never violates that freedom.

7. God may bring a potential mate across your path, but He does not choose that person for you. You make that choice yourself, based on what you learn about that person and on the nature of the friendship that develops.

8. The world builds relationships according to one or more of four basic criteria: physical appearance, social status, intellectual ability, and financial means.

9. The key to finding the right mate is first to identify the qualities and character that we will hold as our standard without compromise, and then evaluate the potential candidates we meet according to those standards.

10. Out of all the people we know, out of all the friendships we develop, out of all the legitimate "possibles" before us, we choose one person with whom we wish to spend the rest of our life.

DISCERNING THE RIGHT LIFE PARTNER

YOUNG PEOPLE IN EVERY SEGMENT OF OUR SOCIETY, AND especially in the Church, need to learn to practice what I call "righteous dating." The word *righteous* in its original concept refers to right positioning, correct alignment, or proper location in relationships. Therefore, righteousness means to be in right alignment with authority, which in the case of a believer, would be God Himself. Righteous dating therefore describes a relationship that is in proper alignment with God and His holy standard, nature, and principles. Righteous relationships are relationships that are in right positioning with God. One of the biggest problems we face in building strong and positive relationships is that the Word of God says one thing, while the example of the world says another. The world trumpets its philosophy everywhere we turn and through every imaginable media; we cannot escape it. God's Word, on the other hand, generally speaks with a much quieter voice. Compounding the problem is the fact that many young believers today are more familiar with the ways of the world than they are with the Word of God. It is no surprise, then, that they are so often confused about how to have a positive dating life that lays the groundwork for a successful marriage.

The primary purpose of dating is to build friendships that help us discern the right life partner. One of the most important principles for successful dating is to get to know the other person by following the proper progression of spirit, soul, and body. Young men and women in the Body of Christ should become acquainted in that order. The first step in any relationship should focus on the spiritual dimension, which is the most important. A couple should take all the time they need to learn where each other stands in matters of faith, worship, and commitment to holy and righteous living as believers. If they cannot agree at the spiritual level, they will have problems at every other level.

After the spiritual comes the "soulical," the level where a couple begins to learn about each other's interests, life purpose, personal and professional goals, education and intellect, and emotional makeup and stability. What do they want out of life? What are their plans for the next year or the next five or ten years? How well do they perform under pressure? They should talk about family, not only the families in which they grew up, but also the family they hope to have someday.

Finally, after a couple have become friends at the spiritual and "soulical" levels, and on the basis of that friendship have decided that they want to spend the rest of their lives together as husband and wife, they move into the physical dimension of their relationship, which is reserved almost exclusively for marriage. At this level, holding hands or sharing a goodnight kiss are acceptable expressions of affection, but anything beyond that is inappropriate until after the wedding.

This progression of spirit, soul, and body is the ticket to a fruitful, satisfying, and successful relationship, but the world flips the whole process upside down. Our modern society recognizes and desires the value of truly fulfilling relationships, but goes after them the wrong way. The model we generally see in the media—movies, television, music, and literature—focuses on the physical aspects of relationship, often to the almost complete exclusion of the "soulical" and the spiritual. Physical union through sex is routinely held up in our culture as the ultimate or standard expression of what it means to be "in love" or "intimate" with another person. Often, it is only after a man and woman have gone to bed together that they attempt to get acquainted in other areas. This is completely contrary to the biblical standard, and helps explain why our modern society is in relational crisis today.

UNDERSTANDING THE STAGES

The spiritual relationship is the first relationship that two people should focus on, with the objective of coming together in one spirit. Spiritual intimacy is achieved when two believers are able to fully and freely share with one another about anything, and particularly God's dealings with them regarding their salvation, total dedication, and victorious Christian living. Anyone who cannot communicate on that level in a dating relationship is already off on the wrong foot.

Dating is a time for a couple to sit down and talk about their spiritual fellowship. Many couples, including many believers, have a problem with this either because they have never been taught that they *should* talk or because they simply don't know what to talk about. Since meaningful conversation does not come easily for many young people, they easily slide into the default mode of getting physical. It starts with a touch, then a kiss, then petting, and one thing leads to another until, almost before they realize it, they have gone farther than they ever intended to go. They step over the line because they could not think of a reason why they shouldn't and because they had no plan in place to keep them from doing so.

> Dating is a time for a couple to sit down and talk about their spiritual fellowship.

Inappropriate physical and sexual behavior while dating generally leads to problems of guilt in marriage that hampers the couple in developing healthy intimacy and, if they are believers, creates difficulty for them in sharing their faith effectively. The only way to avoid that is to stay pure. Those who have already crossed the line into sexual sin can still enter into the purity of Hebrews 9, where it says, "How much more, then, will the blood of Christ, who through the eternal Spirit offered Himself unblemished to God, cleanse our consciences from acts that lead to death, so that we may serve the living God!" (Heb. 9:14). Confession, repentance, and prayer can bring cleansing and a restored purity because the blood of Jesus removes our sin from us as far away as the east is from the west.

God loves us and has our best interests at heart. Because He created us, He knows what is best for us, and His standards of sexual purity and integrity in life are designed to protect us and to ensure that we have rich and fulfilling relationships in accordance with His will.

The "soulical" level is the level of the intellect, the will, and the emotions. Intimacy of soul is achieved as couples begin to make plans for a future together and share their likes and dislikes as they relate to living and working together. A sense of expectation, anticipation, and delight grows as their thoughts center on a definite time when their hopes and plans will be fulfilled. Spiritual oneness leads to an intimate discussion of not only spiritual goals, but personal, intellectual, and physical goals as well.

This level of dreaming and planning is the level where *engagement* takes place. In the days of Jesus, and even before, an engagement was as binding as a marriage. That's why when we read in the Gospel of Matthew of Joseph's discovery that Mary, his betrothed (fiancée), was pregnant, that he planned to *divorce* her quietly. In a sense, an engagement in those days was considered the first stage of marriage, during which the groom prepared a home for his bride and she and her family prepared her dowry and everything else necessary for her moving from her parents' home to her husband's. It was a time during which all of their plans and goals to survive and thrive in their society were laid. During the betrothal, the man and woman were pledged to each other, and the agreement could be broken only by divorce.

In a similar manner, engagement today should be a time for the couple to sit down together and talk about their financial plans, how they are going to live and support themselves, whether they are going to rent an apartment or buy a house, whether they will find employment or go into business for themselves. If either one desires or plans to go to school, this is the time to talk about it, to get everything out in the open so that both are clearly aware of each other's dreams and goals, and so they can plan together to fulfill them.

Engagement should be a serious but joyous time of planning and anticipation. The thoroughness of a couple's planning during engagement will have a significant effect on their future success and happiness in marriage.

Marriage is the gateway into physical union, the third level of relationship. Physical intimacy is consummated in marriage, not before. As it says in the Scripture, "For this reason a man will leave his father and mother and be united to his wife, and they will become one flesh" (Gen. 2:24). The phrase "one flesh" is a sexual reference. Marriage does not bring two spirits together; that occurs at the first level. Neither does it join the minds, wills, and emotions, which takes place at the "soulical" level. Marriage brings a man and a woman together physically; it is essentially sexual in nature. It is designed to meet the physical needs of two people who are already one in spirit and soul.

> Engagement should be a serious but joyous time of planning and anticipation.

This is God's design for relationships. Satan, God's enemy and our adversary, hates this order and always tries to reverse it, because he knows that if he can reverse the order, he can destroy us. Our whole society is built on reversing God's order. Society caters entirely to the physical, not the spiritual. Young people in the Body of Christ cannot get involved in dating without having to deal with this whole issue of the proper order for relationships. Following God's order is the only way to bring about God's results, and God's results are what we are after.

IS HE A CHRISTIAN?

Since there is no one special person that God has for us, and since God does not choose our mate for us, if we are contemplating marriage, we must know how to discern our proper life partner. To discern means to judge astutely based on a standard. Discerning the right life partner is not always easy, particularly if we are confused by the standards of the world. There are a series of questions we can ask about a person we are interested in to help us determine whether or not that person would be a good choice for a mate. Although, for simplicity's sake, these questions and discussions are framed in the masculine gender, they apply equally to females.

The first and most important question of all should be, "Is he a Christian?" This is not the same as asking whether a person is Baptist or Catholic or Pentecostal or Methodist, because there are many people in those and all other denominations as well, who are not genuine believers. Our question is whether or not the person is a Christian. Has he entered into a personal relationship with Jesus Christ as Lord and Savior through faith, repentance, and surrender of life? Is there evidence of that relationship in his behavior and lifestyle? If we wish to be in the will of God in our marriage, then our mate needs to be of the same spiritual persuasion as we are, and walk in the same spirit relationship with God.

> Any person we consider marrying should display continuing evidence of spiritual growth, and so should we.

Behind this question lies a decision and commitment that we will date and marry *only* a believer who is growing in the Lord. None of us are perfect, and no one has reached full maturity but, as believers, we should all be making steady progress on the road to Christlikeness. Any person we consider marrying should display continuing evidence of spiritual growth, and so should we.

A believer marrying an unbeliever is what the apostle Paul calls being "unequally yoked" (2 Cor. 6:14). This is a perfectly clear admonition, yet it never ceases to amaze me how many ways otherwise clearheaded believers find to rationalize their decision to marry an unbeliever. Here are a few that I hear often.

- "He's not a Christian, but he sure is a nice guy." Even nice guys won't make it to Heaven without Jesus. An unbeliever cannot be of the same spirit with a believer because they are not even on the same road together.

- "He's a better gentleman than most Christians I've dated." Polite and respectful behavior is important, but over the long term will not compensate for the absence of spiritual oneness.

- "He's not a Christian because he doesn't want to be a hypocrite." Would he stop going to his bank just because one of the tellers turned out to be a crook? This is merely an excuse to avoid being around believers where he might hear the gospel and get saved.

- "He wants our children to go to my church. That's why I like him." Children in a home where one parent is a believer and one is not often grow up spiritually confused: "Why do I have to go to church? Daddy doesn't go." This is a recipe for trouble.

- "We have so much in common other than religion." At the most basic and fundamental level—the spiritual level—a believer and an unbeliever have nothing in common. The superficial commonalities are inadequate to sustain a relationship with no common spiritual center.

- "I think he's open. Maybe I can witness to him on our dates." Here's the sober, point-blank truth I share with those who rationalize this way: "If he won't change to get you, he won't change to keep you. Once you've lowered your standards to win him, what grounds do you have to try to raise them again afterwards?"

- "I told him he had to be a Christian, so he accepted Christ." If he was sincere, fine, but this raises a question of motivation. Did he "accept Christ" because he knew he needed to be saved, or because he wanted you? Did you tell him he had to be a Christian because you were concerned about his spiritual condition or because you were recruiting a spouse?

Some believers start to panic if they reach a certain age and have not married and see no prospects in sight. Their fear drives them to lower their standards, so that they jump at the first "reasonable" candidate who comes along and shows some interest.

> A believer and an unbeliever have no basis for spiritual intimacy.

No matter how much we try to rationalize, a marriage between a believer and an unbeliever will always be incomplete because the most essential aspect of a total marriage is lost when there is no spiritual union. A believer and an unbeliever have no basis for spiritual intimacy. In this case, discerning the right life partner should be pretty clear. For a believer, an unbeliever is not the right choice for a mate. It's that simple.

WHAT IS MY LIFE GOAL?

The second question we should ask in discerning our life partner is, "What is my life's goal?" It is important that we answer this question before we get involved in a serious relationship, because dating and marriage are directly related to God's purpose in and for our lives. We need first to determine what we want out of life, and then find out what the other person wants out of life to make sure that our life goals are in harmony with each other.

Is there a common commitment to the Kingdom of God? Are we both actively involved in a local fellowship of believers? If we attend different churches, have we agreed on one that we will attend together? Are we of one mind concerning career and professional goals? Are we in agreement concerning if and when we want to have children? Have we shared our personal hopes and dreams with each other so that there will be no surprises later on and so we can be committed together to their fulfillment? Do we pray together regularly, even in public, such as in restaurants before meals?

After the wedding is not the time to discover a discrepancy between each other on these kinds of issues. If he won't pray with you openly before you get married, don't expect him to afterwards. If you want three children but never talk about this with him, don't be surprised if conflict arises over the discovery that he does not want any children.

What are some ways believers rationalize on the life goals issue?

- "When we get married, he will change." Don't count on it. As I have already said, if he won't change to get you, he won't change to keep you. Couples who do not share similar life goals are not right for each other.
- "He's shy about praying or displaying his faith in public." If he is too "shy" to honor Christ publicly, he most likely will not honor Him privately either.

Someone who is bold enough to take a public stand for Christ can be depended on to be faithful to Him in private as well.

- "After we get married, we will get active in church." Maybe so, but probably not. If active involvement in a local fellowship of believers is not a priority before the wedding, don't expect it to be any different after the wedding. Make the commitment now—before the wedding. It will save a lot of grief later.

- "We are only young once." In other words, "We'll become church people after we've had our fling. We're going to live it up now while we are young enough to enjoy it." This rationalization is a sure sign that a couple does not have their life goals clear in their own minds.

- "He's not active in church because another Christian wronged him." Does he stop going to work just because he has an argument with a fellow worker? This is nothing more than an excuse to avoid dealing with a relationship problem. It is a smokescreen to hide the deeper issue—his own estrangement from God.

- "He doesn't come to church because he sees too much hypocrisy there." Isn't it interesting how often the hypocrisy excuse pops up? If he is really so sensitive to hypocrisy in the church, then he needs to come to church to show church people how they should live and act. This is just another smokescreen excuse.

- "I don't want him to think I'm a religious fanatic." What this rationalization actually means is, "If I talk about Jesus too much, I may frighten him away." If he gets frightened about Jesus, he's not the right partner. For a believer, Jesus is the Lord of life and home. Unless both partners love Jesus, there will be trouble.

> Couples who do not share similar life goals are not right for each other.

If a believer marries an unbeliever, they will eventually have conflict because their life goals are not the same. Almost inevitably, a believer who desires to please God will find his or her goals frustrated by the unbelieving spouse. Whether unconsciously or deliberately, the unbelieving partner will try to pull the believing partner away from the Lord. Tragically, I have seen this too many times. I have encountered many frustrated believers who really wanted to obey and follow God, but found their unbelieving mate dragging on them and holding them back. More often than not, the problem stemmed from their failure to sort out the issues of faith and life goals at the beginning.

DOES HE HAVE SELF-CONTROL?

A third consideration in discerning the right life partner is the question, "Does he have self-control?" Is he in command of his temper, his emotions, his passions, and his behavior? Does he exhibit discipline and moderation in all things? Is he careful with money? Does he control his sexual drive, respecting and honoring God's standards limiting sexual expression to the marriage relationship?

First Thessalonians 4:6a says, "In this matter no one should wrong his brother or take advantage of him." The King James Version and several other translations use the word *defraud* for the words *take advantage*. Fraud and defraud are two different words with different meanings. To fraud means to lie and cheat. To defraud means not only to take advantage of someone, but also to be covetous, to overreach, or to make a gain at someone else's expense. With relation to dating, this means that we should never take advantage of anyone we date, or date anyone who will take advantage of us.

This Scripture verse is part of a section in the letter where the apostle Paul warns his readers against the sin of sexual immorality and impurity and calls them to a holy lifestyle. The question of self-control, then, centers mainly around the issue of sexual behavior. This does not mean that self-control is not important in other areas of life. What it does mean is that a person's attitude toward sex is a strong indicator of his attitude in other arenas. A person who lacks self-control in matters of sex will almost certainly exhibit a lack of self-control in other matters as well. One feeds on the other.

Sex is a wonderful gift from God. He created us physically as sexual beings and placed in us all the chemicals and hormones that fuel and fire our sexual drive. He designed the system by which we respond to stimuli and become sexually aroused. God gave all of this to us for our pleasure and enjoyment, provided that we enjoy it within His specified parameters: a committed marriage.

> Someone who exercises self-control in the area of sex
> will also practice self-control in other, less difficult areas.

When we start looking seriously at someone to choose as a life partner, we should make sure that the person we choose understands and respects as we do the boundaries that God has established. Someone who exercises self-control in the area of sex will also practice self-control in other, less difficult areas.

Watch out for this issue. Believers rationalize their behavior (or misbehavior) regarding self-control more often than probably any other area.

- *"I know self-control is important, but what's wrong with our proving that we love each other?"* There are many different ways for couples to show their love for each other without violating each other's self-respect. People who are truly in love will jealously guard each other's self-respect, dignity, and welfare.

- *"He has a few bad habits, but no one is perfect."* If his "bad habit" is that he wants to touch, fondle, and have sex every time you are together, watch out. Ask yourself, "Where did he get this habit?" If it is a habit, he probably picked it up by doing the same thing with other dates. What makes you think he will stop now that he is dating you, or that he will stop after you are married?

- *"He thinks some Christians are too strict."* What he means is, "Your standards are too old-fashioned for today's culture. This is the real world. Lighten up. You need to get in touch with reality." This is really a ploy to get you to give in—to lower yourself to his standards.

- *"Dating standards are different today than they used to be."* Just because "looser" behavior on dates is tolerated today doesn't make it right. As believers, we are committed to God's standards, which never change, because God never changes. He is the same yesterday, today, and forever.

- *"I know we should break up, but I don't want to hurt him."* Which is the wiser choice, to stay in a sinful relationship with an unbeliever, or to walk in the purity of the Spirit and the will of God? Encouraging an unbeliever in his sin will hurt him far more in the long run than will breaking up with him.

Aside from the sinfulness of inappropriate sexual behavior on dates, couples that do not exercise self-control are establishing a dangerous precedent that will carry over into their marriage, even if they end up not marrying each other. Men and women who have sex before marriage are much more likely to be sexually unfaithful to their spouses during marriage than those who do not. Once the pattern is established, it is extremely difficult to break.

There is no victory in compromise. What we are as singles is what we bring into marriage. A very wise and important person in my life told me years ago, "Whatever you compromise to gain, you will lose." How true. Compromising our standards is no way to begin a marriage or any other sustained relationship. We need to learn self-control now, and make sure that any person we consider for a life partner has done the same.

IS THERE HARMONY AT HOME?

One consideration frequently overlooked when examining a potential mate is the question, "Is there harmony at home?" Anyone we consider dating or marrying should be on generally good terms with his own family. How does he get along with his parents and siblings? If he is not welcome at home, it is extremely important to find out why. If his bold stance for Christ has put him at odds with his unbelieving family, that is one thing; if his parents and siblings want nothing to do with him because he treats them like dirt, that is another. Family relations do not have to be perfect, but a deep rift of division or an abundance of anger, bitterness, or hostility are certainly warning flags.

How do people rationalize on this question?

- *"He says I'm the only one he can talk to."* If this is true, he may need professional counseling. More likely, he is unwilling to face his problem realistically or to talk to those involved. Instead, he seeks to drag in someone else who will take his side. Being at odds with a potential spouse's family is not a good way to begin.

- *"I think his parents are too strict."* That may or may not be so, but taking that attitude will likely increase the tension because it will unite the couple against his family in an "us versus them" mentality.

- *"He has a bad temper, but he holds it around me."*
  Most of us are on our best behavior during dates.
  How we act at home says much more about who
  we really are and what we are really like. If he
  loses his temper at home with his parents and
  siblings, eventually he will lose it with the person
  he marries.

- *"Once he leaves home, things will be much better."*
  Don't count on it, particularly if he is the main
  source of the problem. Unresolved conflict transfers. A man tends to treat his wife the same way
  he treats his mother, and a wife tends to respond
  to her husband the same way she responded to
  her father.

Keep in mind also that this question, like all the others, works
both ways. Our own family relations need to be harmonious as
well. Many people get married in order to escape problems or
disharmony at home. That is never a healthy reason to marry.
People whose childhood homes were battlegrounds are likely
to turn their marriage into one as well. Peace begets peace and
strife begets strife. If a couple is at peace with their own closest
relatives, they will bring that peace into their own relationship.

> Unresolved conflict transfers.

IS THIS THE PROPER TIME?

At some point along the way, a couple contemplating marriage
needs to consider the question, "Is this the proper time?" We

should never enter marriage until we are confident that we are in God's will concerning the timing. God will not choose our mate for us, but if we ask Him, He will reveal when the timing is right to marry the person we have chosen.

As believers, we should yield our right to date and to marry to God. Some people have a problem with that idea, especially if they are in their late 20s or early 30s and have not found a likely prospect yet. Our society seems to be in such a rush to make children grow up too fast and push them into dating and other relationships before they are ready. My frequent counsel to young people who are impatient to date or find a boyfriend or girlfriend is, "Relax. Be patient. Settle down and give yourself time to grow first. The more ready you are, the better 'product' they will get, and the more ready they are, the better 'product' you will get."

There are three important questions we should consider to help determine the proper timing: parental consent, financial readiness, and educational goals. Some young people don't want to wait, and say, "Parental consent? Why? We are old enough to make our own decisions." A lot of people get married because of their age rather than because of their character or maturity and end up on a rough road because they are not ready to handle the responsibility of married life. When asked, "Are you financially prepared?" many young, dreamy-eyed couples say, "We'll manage somehow." To the question, "Have you finished all your education?" they reply, "We'll finish school together."

> As believers, we should yield our right to date and to marry to God.

It is important for a couple to receive their parents' consent to get married. Consent is not the same thing as permission. People who are old enough and mature enough to marry do not need their parents' permission to do so. Parental consent, however, can smooth the way considerably for a young couple just starting out. The purpose of seeking parental consent is to ensure that neither set of parents become enemies of the marriage or of the "intruder" who took their child away from them.

I have met few parents who truly and genuinely wanted their child to leave home. The parent-child bond is very strong. Parents have a tendency to hold on tight to their children, even when those children are grown and capable of being on their own. This is precisely what lies behind the Scriptural command: "For this reason a man will leave his father and mother and be united to his wife, and they will become one flesh" (Gen. 2:24). God commands the *children* to *leave*; He does not command the parents to release them.

> The purpose of seeking parental consent is to ensure that neither set of parents become enemies of the marriage or of the "intruder" who took their child away from them.

Because some parents have trouble letting go, there often comes a time when a grown child must say (respectfully), "Mom and Dad, it's time for me to leave home. I have found this wonderful man (or woman) whom I want to marry and spend the rest of my life with. I'm asking for your consent and your blessing. I hope you will give it, but with or without it, I'm getting married." Some parents may have a problem with the idea at first, but they have little choice but to live with it. Parents who deeply desire their child's happiness will do everything they can to ease the transition.

A second consideration as far as timing for marriage is concerned is financial readiness. It amazes me how many couples go into something as serious and long range as marriage with little thought or advance planning as to how they are going to support themselves financially. When asked about this, many couples answer dreamily, "We'll manage somehow," or "We're in love; it will all work out," or "Love will find a way." That is not only foolish and naïve, but is also dangerous.

Whatever you do, *don't* get married with that kind of philosophy. Unless you enter into marriage with a solid financial plan, you are setting yourself up for a lot of heartache and regret down the line. Every married couple needs to start out with money in the bank, a good job (or jobs) with enough income to support them, an investment plan to help them put their money to work and make it grow for them, and a responsible attitude and practice with regard to the use of credit. Establishing *and following* a household budget is also critically important. It is impossible to control and manage your money if you don't know where it is going. Another helpful tool is to have a timeline for your goals as a couple. When do you want to purchase your first house and what do you need to do to get there? What income do you want to have in five years? Ten years? Fifteen years? When do you want to start having children, and what financial preparations do you need to make before enlarging your family?

> Unless you enter into marriage with a solid financial plan, you are setting yourself up for a lot of heartache and regret down the line.

Scientific studies have revealed that financial trouble is the second leading cause of divorce, after sexual problems. Yet, many couples, planning to get married, give little or no thought to financial matters beforehand. If your current financial situation cannot sustain you on your own then the timing is not right for you to get married. Work out your finances first. Know where you are going and how you are going to get there. Don't wait until after the wedding to learn how to manage your money. Learn it now, *before* you "tie the knot."

In addition to parental consent and financial readiness, couples should consider their personal educational goals when determining the timing for getting married. Couples in which one or both are still in high school, listen up—*stay in school! Finish! Graduate! Get your diploma!* Otherwise you are in for a lifetime of struggle and regret. Virtually every employer today, when hiring new workers, expects prospective employees to have a high school diploma *at the very least.*

If you have plans to go to college, then go. Do it now. Don't postpone it to get married first. If you do, the chances are very high that you will never go. Few couples going into marriage fully realize how much marriage will change their lives or how much of a demand it will place on their time and energy and money. Trying to go to college at night while holding down a full-time day job is difficult at best. I know that for two people in love, waiting four years to get married so that one or both can finish college seems like an eternity, but it is nothing compared to the lifetime of regret you will feel if you shortchange your education—and your dreams—by getting married too soon.

> Don't shortchange your education—and your dreams—by getting married too soon.

Parental consent, financial readiness, and educational goals— failure to prepare properly in each of these areas will inevitably cause tension and worry to develop in your marriage, and tension and worry will lead to dangerous stress. Getting married too soon is a sign of impatience, which is a sign of immaturity and of self-love. Self-love is selfish, interested only in getting what it wants and in getting it *now*. True love is always willing to wait because it seeks the absolute best for the other person, desiring that the other person gets every opportunity to attain his or her personal best and to reach his or her highest potential.

WHAT IS MY GIFT?

Finally, in our list of questions to consider in discerning the right life partner is the question, "What is my gift? What do I have that I could contribute to this person?" This involves the conscious decision of yielding our right to date and marry to God. In other words, we say, "Lord, I want to marry in Your will and in Your time and no other. I want to marry when You have confirmed in my heart that I am ready."

Take it from me, when you are ready for marriage, you will know it in an inner "knowing" that has no conflicts. If you apply the questions and principles discussed here, you will also know when you have found the person you want to spend the rest of your life with. Marrying in the will of God carries no inner turmoil or uncertainty because it frees us to concentrate on Christ and His work without distraction. Otherwise, we will stay spiritually immature.

> Marrying in the will of God carries no inner turmoil or uncertainty because it frees us to concentrate on Christ and His work without distraction.

Jesus said it this way:

> *So do not worry, saying, "What shall we eat?" or "What shall we drink?" or "What shall we wear?" For the pagans run after all these things, and your heavenly Father knows that you need them. But seek first his kingdom and his righteousness, and all these things will be given to you as well. Therefore do not worry about tomorrow, for tomorrow will worry about itself. Each day has enough trouble of its own* (Matt. 6:31-34).

In other words, we should preoccupy ourselves with the things of God. God, in turn, will prepare you *for* the one He is preparing for you so that when you both meet, you will both be ready. It is a matter of faith, of trusting in the goodness and faithfulness and trustworthiness of God to meet our every need and fulfill our every dream and desire within the context of His will and timing. It is only when we allow God to fill our deepest needs in His time and in His way that we will know the truest happiness and fulfillment and will be at our most effective in life.

At this stage, we have reached a critical point. We have learned how to know when we are ready to date. We have begun focusing on dating as a time for building friendships. After smashing a couple of common myths regarding finding a mate, we have learned the questions to ask and the principles to consider when discerning the right life partner. When that person comes along—when we have chosen the person we want to marry and that person has, in turn, chosen us—we now enter into the most important premarital stage of all, the stage most critical to ensuring the success of the future marriage. We call this stage *engagement*.

CHAPTER FOUR

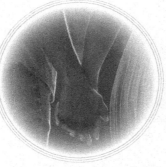

PRINCIPLES

1. The spiritual relationship is the first relationship that two people should focus on, with the objective of coming together in one spirit.

2. Spiritual oneness leads to an intimate discussion of not only spiritual goals, but personal, intellectual, and physical goals as well.

3. Marriage is the gateway into physical union, the third level of relationship.

4. Discerning the right life partner means asking a series of searching questions such as:

    *   Is he a Christian?
    *   What is my life goal?
    *   Does he have self-control?
    *   Is there harmony at home?
    *   Is this the proper time? (i.e., parental consent? Financial readiness? Education completed?)
    *   What is my gift?

ENGAGEMENT: PREPARING TO MARRY

NGAGEMENT, AS A STAGE IN THE PROCESS LEADING TO MAR-riage, is greatly misunderstood in our day and age. By and large, our Western culture generally devalues the importance and significance of engagement as a preparation time for marriage. There was a time when both couples and their parents took engagement very seriously, but those days seem to be fading fast. In the minds of many, with love degraded to little more than sexual activity, and with so many unmarried couples living together and having babies out of wedlock, a formal period of engagement before marriage seems increasingly pointless, a quaint tradition of the past with little contemporary relevance. Indeed, with the institution of marriage itself under such fierce attack in many quarters, a formal period of preparation beforehand appears to many as all but meaningless.

The traditional view of engagement as serious business is well-founded in history. It is only in the last couple of generations that engagement has been all but dismissed as irrelevant. Modern society seems always on the lookout for new trends to follow and new standards by which to measure customs, attitudes, and behavior. As believers and followers of Christ, however, our standard is the Bible, the unchanging Word of God. The Bible takes engagement very seriously, and for that reason we should too.

Many people, including many Christian believers, have little or no understanding of the biblical view of engagement. They understand neither its meaning nor its purpose. They have no real clue as to what to do during engagement, or even why they should bother.

In modern Western culture, engagement is not a serious thing. This is because many people today, particularly those of the youngest generations, are afraid of commitment. They don't want to be "tied down." This fear transfers over into their view of engagement. Two people get engaged and if it doesn't work out they simply split up, find somebody else, and try again. Most of us view engagement as a "trial period," a chance to "test the waters" before plunging into the deep ocean of marriage. As far as society is concerned, nothing is truly binding about engagement; nothing is really etched in stone. In many ways, breaking an engagement is as easy as breaking a date.

The Bible sees it differently. God created the human race. He created us as male and female and instituted marriage as the basic foundation stone of society and as the primary means of a man and a woman relating to each other on an intimate level.

The New Testament reveals that marriage is a symbol, a picture both of the relationship that exists between Jesus Christ and His people, His Church, as well as that which exists in Heaven between the Father, the Son, and the Holy Spirit. Contrary to what many people today believe or assume, marriage was not invented by man but was established by God. As such, it predates law, whether human or divine, as well as every other social or cultural institution.

> Biblical engagement was a binding arrangement, a contractual covenant that could be broken only by divorce.

It stands to reason, then, that something as important as marriage should not be entered into lightly or without adequate preparation. Accordingly, the Bible takes the engagement period very seriously, much more so than we do in our modern society. In the Bible, engagement was not something that people slipped into and out of as easily as they did a coat. Biblical engagement was a binding arrangement, a contractual covenant that could be broken only by divorce.

ENGAGEMENT: THE FIRST STAGE OF MARRIAGE

In addition to being an important time of preparation for marriage, engagement was, in effect, the first stage of marriage. Biblical people who were engaged were regarded as already married, although not to the fullest degree. Full consummation of the marriage, such as living together and sexual union, did not occur until after the wedding ceremony and celebration. The engagement period, which traditionally lasted up to a year, was a time for both the man and the woman to make practical preparations for joining themselves to each other in the fullness of the marriage relationship.

Engagement was contract time, when the families of the couple came together and formally established the marriage covenant, agreeing to release their children to each other. This was much more than the man and woman simply saying to each other, "I commit myself to you." A binding contract was involved that could be terminated only by formal dissolution through divorce.

Things are very different today, although we still maintain a vestigial link to the past through the tradition of the man giving the woman an engagement ring as a symbol of his commitment to marry her. At the wedding, a second ring, the wedding ring, is given as a symbol of exclusive commitment to each other for life in the marriage covenant. The engagement ring is a remnant, a reminder of the way things used to be, of a time when engagement was a much more serious affair than it is today.

Nowadays engaged couples break up all the time. All a fellow has to do is say to the young lady, "I want my ring back." The young lady also can initiate the breakup by simply returning the ring. Usually there are many tears and a lot of hurt. A broken engagement can be very traumatic for both people because engagement was never designed to be terminated so easily.

In biblical days, an engaged man could not simply "ask for his ring" back. A betrothed couple could not simply break off their engagement as though it had never existed. Only a divorce could terminate the relationship. In that event the woman, even if she was still a virgin, would be considered a divorced woman and her fiancé, a divorced man. Divorce carried serious social implications in those days, especially for the woman, just as it did throughout history and up to our own day until the last two or three generations.

> God takes engagement seriously, and believing couples should do the same.

Couples who are contemplating marriage and who want to marry and live within the context of God's Word and His will should consider their engagement as a critical and indispensable time of preparation. Although it is a time of excitement and anticipation, it is also a very serious step, one not to be entered into flippantly or broken off lightly. God takes engagement seriously, and believing couples should do the same.

GOD'S VIEW OF ENGAGEMENT: OLD TESTAMENT

The Book of Deuteronomy contains some very interesting scriptures that illustrate the seriousness of engagement as a stage of marriage. For example, consider these verses from the 22nd chapter:

> *If a man happens to meet in a town a virgin pledged to be married and he sleeps with her, you shall take both of them to the gate of that town and stone them to death—the girl because she was in a town and did not scream*

for help, and the man because he violated another man's wife. You must purge the evil from among you. But if out in the country a man happens to meet a girl pledged to be married and rapes her, only the man who has done this shall die. Do nothing to the girl; she has committed no sin deserving death. This case is like that of someone who attacks and murders his neighbor, for the man found the girl out in the country, and though the betrothed girl screamed, there was no one to rescue her. If a man happens to meet a virgin who is not pledged to be married and rapes her and they are discovered, he shall pay the girl's father fifty shekels of silver. He must marry the girl, for he has violated her. He can never divorce her as long as he lives (Deut. 22:23-29).

In the first scenario, in verse 23, a man meets in town "a virgin pledged to be married"—an engaged woman—and sleeps with her. The penalty for both of them is death by stoning, the same penalty as for adultery. Even though the woman is only "pledged to be married," verse 24 refers to her as "another man's wife." Even though she was only engaged, under the law and custom of the day she was considered already married to the man to whom she was pledged. Her failure to cry out for help implies that the sex was consensual, thereby making her, as well as the man, guilty of adultery. Adultery only applies to married people.

Verses 25-27 show a different scenario in which the woman who is "pledged to be married" is taken by another man while in the country. In this case, the offense is rape and only the man is put to death. The "betrothed" woman is given the benefit of the doubt in the assumption that she screamed for help but no one heard her because she was in the country rather than in a town.

The final example shows the contrast in the penalties for raping an engaged woman and one who is not engaged. In the former case, the man is put to death; in the latter, he must pay the woman's father fifty shekels of silver and marry her. Because he violated her, the law forbids him from ever divorcing her.

Clearly, in the eyes of the Mosaic law, which was handed down from God to Moses, violating an engaged woman was worse than violating one who was not engaged. Thus, we see the serious attitude that God takes, not only about engagement, but also about divorce. An engaged woman who commits sexual sin is guilty of adultery just as if she were "fully" married. God sees engagement as the same as marriage because the penalties for violating them are the same and the requirement for breaking them—divorce—is the same.

What implications does this have for engaged couples today? For one thing, if God takes engagement this seriously, then engaged couples should also. This means that they are committed to one another in a singular and exclusive way, just as if they were already married, except that they are not yet free to have sexual relations.

> As long as your engagement stands, you have a commitment to faithfulness to your fiancée that is as strong and as binding as if he or she was already your spouse.

Someone might ask the question, "If we are engaged, can we still go out with other people?" It depends on the circumstances. For example, if you are engaged and are invited to lunch by someone at work and others from your office will be there, such as a general office luncheon, there's no problem. If someone of the opposite sex at work invites you to lunch tête-à-tête, however, you should decline because you are committed to another. Even if nothing romantic or sexual is implied or intended, you should decline to avoid any appearance of impropriety. Even though you are not yet married, your engagement has taken you beyond singleness and into the *realm* of marriage. As long as your engagement stands, you have a commitment to faithfulness to your fiancée that is as strong and as binding as if he or she was already your spouse. In that sense, the marriage has already begun. That's the way the Word of God sees it.

JESUS BORN OUT OF WEDLOCK?

Another biblical example of the close relation between engagement and marriage is seen in the circumstances surrounding the birth of Jesus Christ Himself. One of the central confessions of traditional Christian faith is that Jesus was born of a virgin. At the time of Jesus' birth Mary, His mother, was a virgin, having never known a man sexually. She was, however, engaged to a man named Joseph. As Matthew, one of the New Testament Gospel writers, relates:

> *A record of the genealogy of Jesus Christ the son of David, the son of Abraham:… and Jacob the father of Joseph, the husband of Mary, of whom was born Jesus, who is called Christ…. This is how the birth of Jesus Christ came*

about: His mother Mary was pledged to be married to Joseph, but before they came together, she was found to be with child through the Holy Spirit. Because Joseph her husband was a righteous man and did not want to expose her to public disgrace, he had in mind to divorce her quietly. But after he had considered this, an angel of the Lord appeared to him in a dream and said, "Joseph son of David, do not be afraid to take Mary home as your wife, because what is conceived in her is from the Holy Spirit. She will give birth to a son, and you are to give him the name Jesus, because he will save his people from their sins." All this took place to fulfill what the Lord had said through the prophet: "The virgin will be with child and will give birth to a son, and they will call him Immanuel"—which means, "God with us." When Joseph woke up, he did what the angel of the Lord had commanded him and took Mary home as his wife. But he had no union with her until she gave birth to a son. And he gave him the name Jesus (Matt. 1:1,16,18-25).

Verse 16 refers to Joseph as the "husband of Mary," the mother of Jesus. Mary herself is described in verse 18 as "pledged to be married to Joseph." The King James Version says she was "espoused" to Joseph. "Engaged" is our modern word. Although she was a virgin, Mary was found to be pregnant by the Holy Spirit. Does this mean that Jesus was born "out of wedlock"? Strictly speaking, perhaps, yes. After all, His mother, Mary, was not married when He was born. Neither was she single, however. She was betrothed or pledged to Joseph. In the eyes of the law and the culture of that day, the two of them were regarded as husband and wife even though they were still in the betrothal period and had not yet begun their life together as a married couple in the fullest sense.

In a broader sense, however, Jesus was not born out of wedlock. His conception in Mary's womb was an entirely supernatural act with nothing remotely sexual about it. It was a true miracle, in which God overrode and transcended the normal human, physical process of procreation in order to bring His Son into the world. Such an event had no connection whatsoever with the normal cycle of engagement and marriage.

When Joseph learned of Mary's pregnancy, he very naturally assumed that she had violated her betrothal, her engagement to him. His response reveals a great deal about his character. He could have hauled her into the open and shamed her publicly by branding her an adulteress. Potentially, she could have been stoned. Instead Joseph, wanting to spare Mary the hardship, humiliation, and public disgrace, decided to divorce her secretly. They were only engaged. The wedding ceremony had not occurred, they were not living together, and had not yet entered into a full marriage relationship, yet divorce was the only way for Joseph to break off their engagement.

ENGAGEMENT IS THE BEGINNING OF MARRIAGE

Hebrews 13:8 says, "Jesus Christ is the same yesterday and today and forever." The same is true of God the Father, since He and Jesus are of the same essence. This means that God never changes. He is absolutely constant and consistent in every way.

What was true of Him 2,000, 4,000, or 6,000 years ago is still true of Him today. If engagement was a serious matter to Him in Mary and Joseph's day, then it is a serious matter to Him in our own generation and therefore should be a serious matter to all of us.

Thanks be to God for His grace through the Lord Jesus Christ, who has given us freedom from the penalty of the law. Otherwise, we might still be facing stoning for breaking it. Jesus cancelled the penalty for our sin and our law-breaking when He went to the cross. Although we have been set free from the law and now live by grace through faith, we still have the responsibility to know and observe the spirit of the law not by our own strength or works, but in the power of the Holy Spirit who lives inside every believer.

For this reason, we should view engagement the same way and with the same seriousness as God does. Engagement is the *beginning* of marriage, the first stage in the marriage relationship. This does not mean it is alright for engaged people to sleep together. The physical consummation of the marriage is reserved for after the wedding when the marriage, in its fullness, begins. Note that even though Joseph and Mary were engaged and considered to be in the first stage of marriage, they did not come together in sexual union until after Jesus was born and after they had solemnized their wedding vows.

Engagement is the period when the marriage covenant is established between a man and a woman. It is a time for deepening the friendship and spiritual oneness that they should have developed during their time of dating, as well as a time for growing in the practical, mental, and emotional areas—the "soulical" part of their relationship. During engagement, the couple should be learning to think and act as one in anticipation of the day when, after the wedding, they consummate their union by joining together physically to become "one flesh."

The Bible makes a distinction between being single and being engaged just as it does between being single and being married. Engagement is an intermediate stage where a man and a woman are committed fully to each other, no longer uncommitted, or unattached, but not yet married in the fullest sense either.

A common attitude among engaged couples today is, "We're just testing the waters. That's why we're engaged. We want to see if our relationship will work out." Engagement is not the time for testing the waters. That's what the dating period is for. By the time a couple reaches the engagement stage, they should already have tested the waters. They should already know whether or not their relationship is going to work out. Their engagement should not be a trial period but a public testimony stating, "We have chosen each other to join together in marriage for life. We are now in a time of making practical preparations to ensure that when the wedding day comes, we will be ready in every way to help guarantee our success."

> Engagement is not the time for testing the waters. That's what the dating period is for.

This practical planning and preparation stage is the phase of their relationship where Joseph and Mary were when Joseph learned that she was pregnant. Before he could carry out his plan to divorce her, however, Joseph had a dream in which an angel of

God appeared and explained everything to him. Mary had not been unfaithful to Joseph. She had not violated her betrothal to him. The child in her womb had been conceived by the Holy Spirit and would grow up to be God's Deliverer, the Savior and Messiah of His people. Joseph, therefore, should not be afraid to take Mary as his wife. She had remained faithful to him and they had been chosen by God—together—to nurture and raise God's Son.

Heeding to the angel's counsel, Joseph did take Mary as his wife. Together they completed their preparation time and solemnized their marriage covenant, but refrained from sexual relations until after Jesus was born. Joseph was already a conscientious and righteous man. I wonder how this news of becoming the earthly father of the Messiah affected Joseph's attitude toward the remainder of his preparation time! Now he had an even stronger motivation than before to prepare a good home and be ready to receive Mary as his wife. Very soon they would have a son to care for.

Marriage in the Bible began with engagement, which is why a divorce was required in order to break it. Sexual union, however, did not begin with the engagement but was reserved for after the wedding. Full consummation could take place only after the marriage was fully solemnized.

Because God's Word never changes, the same standards apply to engagement today. Unfortunately, many people today, including many believers, are confused on this issue. They say, "Well, since we're engaged and are going to be married anyway, we might as well go all the way." Studies show that more and more engaged couples start having sex before they reach the marriage altar. Many of them are becoming sexually active even earlier, before they meet their future spouse and become engaged. Although this is becoming more common, it is a serious mistake and is very dangerous to the future health of any marriage relationship.

Marriage is the consummation of engagement, the climax of all the planning and all the dreams, and all the thoughts, and all the hopes and aspirations that the couple has shared with each other. Any sexual union before marriage is sin—the Bible calls it fornication—and if it involves an engaged person, it is adultery.

Godly marriage is a covenant. Engagement is the beginning of that covenant and marriage is the consummation of it. When we become engaged to a person, we are telling that person, "I am committed to you. I am entering into covenant with you to be yours exclusively and for you to be mine exclusively for as long as life shall last." That is why we refrain from sexual activity during that time. We want to honor and protect our marriage covenant, and the way we do that is by keeping ourselves pure.

ENGAGEMENT AND MARRIAGE CUSTOMS IN BIBLICAL DAYS

How were engagements and weddings carried out in biblical days? Unfortunately, the Bible itself gives us very few details regarding engagement customs or wedding practices and ceremonies. Some non-biblical writings from the same period, however, do offer some clues. Ancient writings from people such as the Jewish historian Josephus and others, some even as far back as Old Testament times, have left written records that contain some information about certain aspects of the engagement period and the wedding as they were practiced in that day and in that culture. It is reasonable to believe that the people in the Bible followed the same practices and customs.

One brief account is found in the apocryphal book of Tobit. The Apocrypha is the name given to a collection of ancient Jewish writings that Catholics include as part of the Old Testament but that most other Christians do not accept as God-inspired Scripture. Their primary importance lies in the information they provide regarding the history as well as the spiritual, moral, and ethical climate of Palestine during the years between the end of the Old Testament period and the beginning of the New Testament period.

Tobit is a folktale that dates around 200 B.C. and tells of a devout Jew living in Nineveh named Tobit who has become blind. Tobit sends his son Tobias to collect a deposit of money he had left in another city. Along the way, Tobias is assisted by the angel Raphael who provides him with a magic formula that can heal Tobit's blindness. Tobias also meets and falls in love with a beautiful young woman named Sarah, who has had seven husbands, each one killed by a demon on their wedding night. Despite this gruesome history, Tobias marries Sarah anyway and with Raphael's help, drives away the demon. Eventually, Tobias returns home with his wife, his father's money, and a formula that restores his father's sight.

The section of the story where Tobias marries Sarah reveals some things about the customs surrounding marriage in those days. Tobias and Raphael, who is posing as an Israelite named Azarias, are seated at dinner with Raguel, Sarah's father:

After they had taken a bath and washed their hands, and had sat down to dinner, Tobias said to Raphael, "Azarias, my friend, ask Raguel to give me Sarah my kinswoman." Raguel overheard and said to the young man: "Eat, drink, and be happy tonight. There is no one but yourself who should have my daughter Sarah; indeed I have no right to give her to anyone else, since you are my nearest kinsman…I give her to you as the ordinance in the book of Moses prescribes. Heaven has ordained that she shall be yours. Take your kinswoman. From now on, you belong to her and she to you; she is yours forever from this day. The Lord of heaven prosper you both this night, my son, and grant you mercy and peace."

Raguel sent for his daughter Sarah, and when she came he took her hand and gave her to Tobias, saying: "Take her to be your wedded wife in accordance with the law and the ordinance written in the book of Moses. Keep her and take her home to your father; and may the God of heaven keep you safe and give you peace and prosperity." Then he sent for her mother and told her to bring paper, and he wrote out a marriage contract granting Sarah to Tobias as his wife, as the law of Moses ordains. After that they began to eat and drink.

Raguel called his wife and said, "My dear, get the spare room ready and take her in there." Edna went and prepared the room as he had told her, and took Sarah into it. Edna cried over her, then dried her tears and said: "Courage, dear daughter; the Lord of heaven give you joy instead of sorrow. Courage, daughter!" Then she went out.

When they had finished eating and drinking and were ready for bed, they escorted the young man to the bridal chamber (Tobit 7:8-10,12-18;8:1, NEB).[1]

Tobias immediately sets up a potion given to him by Raphael that drives the demon away, after which he and Sarah pray for God's protection and blessing on their lives as husband and wife.

Notice the specific elements related to marriage that are described here. First, there was an agreement between the bride's father and the bridegroom in which the father granted permission for the bridegroom to marry his daughter. Second, the bride's father formally presented her to her bridegroom by giving her to him. Then he pronounced a blessing upon them and upon their union. Next, the father wrote up a marriage contract that made everything official and in accordance with the Law of Moses. The bride was then taken to the bridal chamber where she waited for her new husband to come to her. While she waited, her husband and her father and any others present feasted and celebrated. Finally, after the feasting was done, the bridegroom was led to the bridal chamber where he went into his wife. There they consummated the marriage.

From other ancient sources we learn that a typical betrothal or engagement lasted from nine to twelve months. Its purpose was to give the individuals time to prepare for their marriage. Marriage was too important a matter, too sacred an institution to enter into lightly or flippantly or without adequate preparation. During this time, the parents of the couple drew up the marriage contract, which laid out the terms and conditions for the marriage agreement, including the responsibilities incurred by both families. The terms of the contract had to be certified and fulfilled before the marriage could proceed.

> Marriage is too important a matter, too sacred an institution to enter into lightly or flippantly or without adequate preparation.

For example, the bride's father might stipulate: "Okay, if you want my daughter for your son, here are my terms. By the end of the betrothal period, I want 50,000 shekels, 10 camels and 10 donkeys. I want a finished house paid for and ready for my daughter. She will need two menservants and five maidservants." The groom's father might then respond: "I accept those terms. Now for my son, I want a wife who can cook, sew, weave, wash, and generally run the household. She also needs to be able to bear children so that my son can raise up heirs."

Once the terms of the contract were agreed upon, both parties would sign and it would become official. The modern-day equivalent of this contract, even though we don't hear much about it anymore, is the idea of a dowry that each person, but particularly the bride, brings into the marriage.

After the contract was signed, the formal period of engagement began. For the next nine to twelve months, the bride and groom busied themselves getting ready for each other. The groom went to work earning money so that the 50,000 shekels would be there at the right time. He bought or built a house and fixed it up so it would be ready for his new wife. He had to be a good businessman, a good leader, and a good organizer; a self-controlled man who did not squander his money. During those months of betrothal he had to prepare himself physically, mentally, psychologically, and socially for receiving his bride and making the transition from bachelor to married head of a household.

In the meantime, the bride's mother was making sure her daughter knew how to sew, weave, cook, clean, and keep house. The bride learned how to manage a household budget. At some point, the mother also taught her daughter about the physical and sexual aspects of marriage from a wife's perspective so that the new bride would know what to expect and how to please her husband.

Let's be honest now. Don't you think that if couples in our day and age would return to some kind of formal agreement like this when they became engaged that they would avoid many of the problems that are so common to newlyweds? So many couples today go into marriage with little or no financial preparation. They don't know where they are going to live or even how they are going to make a living. Even before they become financially stable they have a baby, then another, then another, with no plan and no clue how to provide for them.

Think what a difference it would make if the young lady's father sat down with the young man and said, "If you want to marry my daughter with my blessing, here is what I expect from you…" and then give him a list of the things he needs to do to demonstrate that he is ready to marry the girl. Check the fellow out. How does he plan to support her? Does he have a good, steady job? Where will they live? An apartment? A condo? A house of their own? Any responsible father wants to ensure that his daughter is going to be taken care of and treated well by the man who marries her.

> Expectations are not as important as understanding and agreeing that both are equally responsible for... everything...that goes into making their marriage work.

At the same time, a prospective husband needs to know that the woman he is marrying has the basic skills necessary to help him run the household and build a successful marriage. Expectations are not as important as understanding and agreeing that both are equally responsible for the home and the relationship, for raising the kids, for money management, and for everything else that goes into making their marriage work.

Of course, in our society, a couple that is of age can marry without their parents' blessing or consent. Sometimes this is unavoidable. If possible, however, it is always better to have the parents' consent and blessing because it helps smooth things along, particularly in the earliest days of the marriage.

A FOURTEEN-YEAR ENGAGEMENT

We live in a day and age characterized by impatience and the demand for instant gratification. Few people are willing to wait anymore. Whatever we want, we want it right now. Many newly married couples today insist on immediately buying a house of their own even if they cannot really afford it. Their reason? "Mom and Dad owned their own home, so why not us?" They never stop to think that Mom and Dad might have had to wait five or ten years or longer before they were ready financially to invest in buying a home.

Many couples today who plan to marry dispense with a long engagement. They don't see the point; they're just anxious to get on with it. If you think you would have a problem waiting through a nine-month engagement, what about 14 years? Would you wait 14 years to get the one you love? Would that person wait 14 years for you?

The Book of Genesis tells the story of how Jacob fell in love with a beautiful woman named Rachel and, in the end, worked for 14 years in order to have her as his wife. Jacob was the son of Isaac and Rebekah. After incurring the murderous wrath of his older brother Esau by cheating him out of both his birthright and his father's blessing for the eldest son, Jacob fled for his life. Eventually, Jacob made his way to his mother's homeland and settled down with the family of her brother, his uncle Laban. It was there that Jacob met Rachel, Laban's younger daughter. He quickly fell in love with her and wanted to marry her. Jacob's story reveals some more information regarding engagement and marriage customs and practices of the day.

> *Jacob was in love with Rachel and said, "I'll work for you seven years in return for your younger daughter Rachel." Laban said, "It's better that I give her to you than to some other man. Stay here with me." So Jacob served seven years to get Rachel, but they seemed like only a few days to him because of his love for her. Then Jacob said to Laban, "Give me my wife. My time is completed, and I want to lie with her." So Laban brought together all the people of the place and gave a feast. But*

when evening came, he took his daughter Leah and gave her to Jacob, and Jacob lay with her. And Laban gave his servant girl Zilpah to his daughter as her maidservant. When morning came, there was Leah! So Jacob said to Laban, "What is this you have done to me? I served you for Rachel, didn't I? Why have you deceived me?" Laban replied, "It is not our custom here to give the younger daughter in marriage before the older one. Finish this daughter's bridal week; then we will give you the younger one also, in return for another seven years of work." And Jacob did so. He finished the week with Leah, and then Laban gave him his daughter Rachel to be his wife. Laban gave his servant girl Bilhah to his daughter Rachel as her maidservant. Jacob lay with Rachel also, and he loved Rachel more than Leah. And he worked for Laban another seven years (Gen. 29:18-30).

Jacob entered into a contract with Laban under which he would work for his uncle for seven years in return for receiving Rachel as his wife. Laban proved to be as much of a schemer and deceiver as Jacob himself. After the seven years were completed and Jacob asked for Rachel, Laban tricked him by marrying him to Leah, his older daughter.

How could such a thing have happened? How was Jacob deceived into marrying the wrong woman? It is not so hard to understand when we remember the customs of the day. First of all, Jacob would have had very little physical contact with Rachel during those seven years and absolutely no contact that was sexual in nature. Second, at the time of the wedding ceremony, the bride's face was completely covered by an opaque veil that would be removed only by her husband when they were alone together in the bridal chamber. Third, after the wedding ceremony, as we saw with Tobias and Sarah, the bride was taken to the bridal chamber to wait for her new husband. Only after many hours of feasting and celebrating would the husband join his wife in the tent. By that time it was completely dark, and the husband and wife would not even see each other's faces until the next morning.

Because of these customs, Jacob had no reason to know that he did not have Rachel until he saw the face of Leah in the morning light. Greatly angered at the deception, Jacob confronted Laban, who simply explained that it was not customary to marry off the younger daughter before the older daughter. Laban struck another deal with Jacob. After Jacob finished the bridal week with Leah, Laban gave him Rachel in marriage in return for another seven years of work. Jacob agreed to the terms because of his love for Rachel.

It is important to note that Jacob did not have to work the additional seven years *before* he married Rachel. He worked them afterwards to meet the conditions set by her father. Had he not done so, Laban could have taken Rachel away and probably would have done so. In effect, then, Jacob had a 14-year engagement period. He invested 14 years of his life in order to have the woman he loved. The fact that seven of those years came after he married her is immaterial. They were still conditions he had to meet.

Schemer though he was, Laban was looking out for the welfare of his daughters. He put Jacob to work at least partly so that his daughters would not be married to a man who was broke.

During the 21 years that Jacob worked for Laban (seven each for his two wives and seven additional years to build up his own flocks and herds) Jacob become very prosperous. The Lord blessed him so that he became as rich as his uncle. When Jacob finally left Laban and took his family and livestock back to his own homeland, he was a very wealthy man.

ENGAGEMENT: A TIME TO SECURE MARRIAGE STABILITY

Jacob's experience is probably rather unique; few people are ever in his position of having to work 14 years for the woman he loves. His story illustrates the fact that engagement is not a time of idleness and "pie-in-the-sky-by-and-by" dreaming, but a period of hard work and preparation. When Jacob and his family left Laban's house, they took with them everything Jacob had acquired during his time there. Those 21 years prepared him thoroughly to provide for his wives and children in every way. His time of preparation helped secure and ensure the success and stability of his marriage and family.

> Engagement is not a time of idleness and "pie-in-the-sky-by-and-by" dreaming, but a period of hard work and preparation.

That is where the lesson lies for us today. Contrary to the way many couples treat it, the engagement period is a time to secure the stability of the upcoming marriage. Most unsuccessful marriages fail because of issues that could have and should have been addressed during the engagement. Finances, housing, sexual needs and expectations, parenting philosophy, educational dreams and goals—all of these are potential trouble spots for married couples. Trouble can be avoided or at least minimized simply by discussing and working through these issues before the wedding so that both parties have a full and complete understanding and are in agreement with each other.

> Most unsuccessful marriages fail because of issues that could have and should have been addressed during the engagement.

Engagement is a time of preparation for marriage. Note that I did not say a time of preparation for the wedding. Certainly wedding planning needs to take place during that time, but that is not the primary purpose of the engagement period. Many couples make the mistake of planning only for the wedding and thinking very little about what follows.

A wedding is an event, but marriage is a life. A wedding lasts only a brief time but a marriage lasts "until death do us part." Where is the wisdom in spending $500.00 on a wedding dress, $10,000.00 on the wedding, $5,000.00 on the reception, but not a single penny on books or counseling or other resources on how to make a marriage? An engagement devoted solely to planning for a 30-minute ceremony is wasted time. Much more important is time spent getting ready for the marriage; preparing for a lifetime with the person you have chosen and who has chosen you.

> A wedding is an event, but marriage is a life.

Paul gave this counsel to the believers in Ephesus:

Be very careful, then, how you live—not as unwise but as wise, making the most of every opportunity, because the days are evil. Therefore do not be foolish, but understand what the Lord's will is (Eph. 5:15-17).

Although Paul is speaking primarily about the proper way believers should live, his counsel applies just as well to engaged couples. Make the most of your opportunity *before* the wedding to prepare yourselves for the marriage that follows. Verse 16 in the King James Version reads, "Redeeming the time, because the days are evil."

Don't waste your engagement period on daydreaming and flights of fancy or naïvely assuming, "We're in love; everything will work out." Redeem the time—use your time wisely to consider, plan, think through, and discuss every aspect of your upcoming life together. Success in marriage does not come by accident but only through careful planning. The time to plan for success is not after you say, "I do," but long before you stand at the altar. The time to plan for a successful marriage is during your engagement.

Note

1 *The New English Bible.* (New York: Cambridge University Press, 1972.)

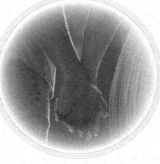

PRINCIPLES

1. Engagement is a critical and indispensable time of preparation for marriage.

2. An engaged couple is committed to each other in a singular and exclusive way, just as if they are already married, except that they are not yet free to have sexual relations.

3. Engagement is the beginning of marriage, the first stage in the marriage relationship.

4. Engagement is the period when the marriage covenant is established between a man and a woman.

5. Godly marriage is a covenant. Engagement is the beginning of that covenant and marriage is the consummation of it.

6. The engagement period is a time to secure the stability of the upcoming marriage.

7. The time to plan for a successful marriage is during your engagement.

ENGAGEMENT: REDEEMING THE TIME

AS A VITAL PREPARATION TIME FOR MARRIAGE, THE ENGAGE-ment period is too important to waste on inconsequential matters. Many engaged couples do little more during that time than plan the wedding and perhaps talk in generalities about work and career plans. It is quite common for couples to wait until they are engaged to talk specifically about their goals. While this is better than not talking about them at all, engagement is not really the time for such a discussion. Courtship is the time for couples to talk about their goals and objectives, their dreams and desires, and to plan their future. By the time a couple reaches the engagement stage, all these things should be in place. They should know where they want to go, how they plan to get there, and should have a oneness of heart and spirit to go there together.

Engagement is the time for couples to put into place and execute their action plan to get them where they want to go. It is a time to move from planning to walking determinedly together in the same direction. One definition of the word "engage" is "to interlock with," or "mesh together," and the word "engagement," the state of being "in gear." By the time a couple becomes engaged, their goals, objectives, dreams, desires, and values should interlock with each other and mesh together as one, and they should be "in gear" with each other as they move forward with their practical preparations to bring those things to pass.

> Engagement is the time for couples to put into place and execute their action plan to get them where they want to go.

I counsel young couples to use their engagement period to develop a 50-year life plan, a plan that lays out where they want to go, what they want to do, and what they want to become over the next 50 years. Of course, it is impossible for anyone to predict with complete accuracy the direction his or her life will take over a 50-year period. Unanticipated life changes and unexpected opportunities will almost certainly come along that could lead to a change in direction. Some goals may be reached and some plans come to fruition sooner than expected while others may be dropped altogether. Any such life plan therefore needs to have built-in flexibility to allow for the unexpected. The important thing is for engaged couples to have a plan, a "road map" to guide them over the months and years of marriage that lie ahead and to help them stay on course to reach their dreams and goals and avoid getting sidetracked onto dead ends or other paths that will take them where they don't want to go.

For some folks, engagement means going out for ice cream, going to movies, holding hands, kissing, and such. That's not engagement; that's dating. Of course, engaged couples do those kinds of things because they continue dating, but engagement involves much more than that; it goes much deeper.

Engagement is hard-core planning, where a couple gets down to the brass tacks of preparing for life after the wedding. This is where, depending on their circumstances, they go looking for an apartment to rent or a house to buy or a plot of land on which to build. They talk to real estate agents and house contractors. They visit banks to check out car loans. They set money back in savings against future expenses. They consider and anticipate every possible snag or glitch or obstacle they can think of and provide for those possibilities in advance. The goal is to have everything so well in order by the end of the engagement period that, from the start their marriage, everything will run like a well-oiled machine.

There are several key areas that engaged couples should focus their attention on during this all-critical period of engagement. Proper care and preparation given to these things now will smooth the transition into married life and make things a lot easier down the line. Any couples seeking to ensure a healthy and successful marriage should give due attention to a spiritual foundation, economic stability, educational goals, parenting philosophy, and sexual standards. Together, these five areas comprise the categories where virtually all marital problems and divisions occur. Getting "in gear" with each other now on these issues will help avoid problems later on.

A SPIRITUAL FOUNDATION

Every believing couple should lay a strong, solid, spiritual foundation for their marriage during their engagement. Don't wait until after the wedding. So many things are going on in the aftermath of a wedding and making the adjustment to married life that securing a solid spiritual foundation can be easily shoved aside.

By spiritual foundation I am not talking about determining whether or not each partner is a believer. That should have been established during the dating (courtship) phase. If it was not, then by all means take care of it now. No single area is more important for future marital success than for a couple to make sure they are "in gear" spiritually, that they see eye to eye on spiritual matters.

Among other things, laying a solid spiritual foundation means coming into agreement about where they will go to church: his church? her church? a "neutral" church as a compromise? Agreeing on one church that they will attend together is important for the sake of spiritual harmony in the home as well as helping to prevent spiritual confusion in the minds of the children later on. "Mommy, why do we have to go to church? Daddy doesn't." "Daddy, why does Mommy go to a different church than we do?" This is also why it is important for a couple to make the commitment beforehand to regular attendance and active involvement in Bible study, praise and worship, preaching, and ministry and service in whatever local fellowship of believers they choose.

No single area is more important for future marital success than for a couple to make sure they are "in gear" spiritually, that they see eye to eye on spiritual matters.

Laying a strong spiritual foundation also means under-standing and recognizing the God-given role of the man as the spiritual leader (not dictator!) of the home under the over-all Lordship of Jesus Christ. The man must be willing to accept this responsibility. Both partners must make a mutual commit-ment to building a strong Christian home.

The Bible clearly indicates that a firm spiritual foundation is the most important aspect in building a healthy marriage and family life. Moses gave the Israelites these instructions shortly before they crossed the Jordan River into the land of Canaan:

> *Hear, O Israel: The Lord our God, the Lord is one. Love the Lord your God with all your heart and with all your soul and with all your strength. These commandments that I give you today are to be upon your hearts. Impress them on your children. Talk about them when you sit at home and when you walk along the road, when you lie down and when you get up* (Deut. 6:4-7).

Parents were charged not only to obey God's commands themselves, but to teach their children to obey them as well. This requires a firm spiritual foundation in the home. Our soci-ety today is plagued by the *laissez-faire*, or "hands-off," attitude many parents have toward the spiritual lives of their children: "We don't want to pressure them to accept our beliefs. They need to make their own decisions." Indeed, everyone must make a personal choice regarding spiritual matters, but that does not relieve us as parents of our God-given responsibil-ity to teach our children our beliefs and values. Children must make their own choices, yes, but they deserve the opportunity to make an informed choice. How can they do that unless we teach them?

Scripture also warns of the spiritual dangers to the marriage and family life of believers being "unequally yoked" with unbelievers. As we noted in chapter four, a believer should not marry an unbeliever. That kind of union makes it impossible to build a solid spiritual foundation, because the unbelieving partner lacks the necessary spiritual frame of reference. Paul told the Corinthian believers, "Do not be yoked together with unbelievers. For what do righteousness and wickedness have in common? Or what fellowship can light have with darkness?" (2 Cor. 6:14). Through Moses, God gave a similar warning to the Israelites before they entered the land of Canaan. Referring to the pagan peoples who inhabited the land, Moses said, "Do not intermarry with them. Do not give your daughters to their sons or take their daughters for your sons, for they will turn your sons away from following me to serve other gods, and the Lord's anger will burn against you and will quickly destroy you" (Deut. 7:3-4).

Although the primary focus of these verses is on the danger of believers marrying unbelievers, the same principle applies in emphasizing the importance of two believers who are engaged or married being in spiritual harmony and agreement with each other.

Spiritual harmony promotes oneness, which is one vital characteristic couples should develop during their engagement. Oneness is at the heart of what Jesus desires for His children. His prayer to His Father the night before He was crucified was a prayer for all of us:

My prayer is not for them alone. I pray also for those who will believe in me through their message, that all of them may be one, Father, just as you are in me and I am in you. May they also be in us so that the world may believe that you have sent me. I have given them the glory that you gave me, that they may be one as we are one: I in them and you in me. May they be brought to complete unity to let the world know that you sent me and have loved them even as you have loved me (John 17:20-23).

"Complete unity," or oneness, is Christ's desire for His people, and that includes believing couples, either married or soon to be married. Oneness is the glue that holds a relationship together. Without this sense of oneness, a marriage relationship will gradually start breaking up into "his" and "her" segments: separate bank accounts, separate goals, separate visions, separate beds and finally, separate lives. Lack of oneness is a sure sign of trouble in the relationship, and one of the best ways to build oneness is to be in spiritual harmony and agreement with each other. The ideal time to build oneness and spiritual harmony is during engagement.

Oneness is the glue that holds a relationship together.

ECONOMIC STABILITY

Next to spiritual matters, economic and financial issues probably cause more marital problems than any other area. Continual disagreements over money or financial management practices cause serious hurt and injury to any relationship. A couple entering marriage with no financial plan is headed for trouble from the start. After the wedding is not the time for a couple to discover that their current income is not enough to buy groceries, put gas in the car, pay the light bill and pay the rent for the apartment they just moved into. The morning after their first night as husband and wife is not the time for her to hear him say, "Well, I guess I better go look for a job."

Issues such as these should be settled during engagement, *long* before the wedding day. That may sound like a "no-brainer" statement, but you would be amazed at the number of engaged couples I encounter who give almost no thought to these things. They just go merrily along day by day, blithely ignoring or blissfully unaware of the economic and financial realities of married life. Many of them discover too late that two people cannot live as cheaply as one. Too late they learn that wise financial planning is much harder to do "on the run," amidst all the adjustments and obligations of married life, than to sit down beforehand and chart the financial course of their lives.

Long before they say "I do," couples should discuss and nail down the financial strategy they will take into their marriage. Will the husband alone work outside the home, or will both husband and wife work? If employed, are one or both beyond the standard probationary period, or will be by the time of the wedding? Will they work a job as an employee of someone else or will they start their own business? If they plan to start their own business, do they have the financial capital to do so immediately? If not, how will they acquire the capital? Will they borrow it? Will they seek investors to partner with them in the venture? Will they work a "regular" job for a while, saving every penny they can until they have the capital they need to break out on their own?

Where will they live? How much can they afford to pay? Will they rent an apartment? Will they buy a house? Will they build a house? If buying or building, which banks offer the lowest interest rates and the best service? Will they live in the city or in the suburbs, on the beach or along the freeway?

How many cars will they drive and what kind? Will they be new or used? Can they get by with one or will they need two? Can they afford the insurance for their vehicles? What kind of health care coverage will they have? How will they pay for it, especially if they are self-employed?

How will they make their money grow and work for them? What is their investment plan? Do they *have* an investment plan? How often will they invest and at what amount? What is their financial plan for retirement? Do they have one? Do they have a family budget? Does it allow a reasonable amount for personal allowances, including leisure and recreation? Are they willing and prepared to pool their money into joint bank accounts? How will they handle "extra" money—gifts, bonuses, overtime, tax refunds, inheritances, et cetera?

If one or both are still in school, do they have a practical plan for finishing? Do they have a financial strategy in place to ensure that they can finish?

Singleness, or oneness, of purpose and goal is just as important in the economic arena as in the spiritual. Couples need to work together and be equally knowledgeable about the financial affairs of the household because they are partners in marriage, not simply two individuals living in the same house. They need to be in mutual agreement about how and when and on what they will spend their money. More often than not, this will involve agreeing together on general principles, and those principles will then be used to guide each specific situation. Nothing can start a financial argument faster than the discovery that one partner spent money outside the agreed-upon guidelines without discussing it with the other partner first.

One of the most frustrating things I have run into is couples who don't know what to do with the economic life they have. The husband and wife live in two different worlds. I have met some husbands who are *ashamed* that their wives know how much they make! These are folks who have been married for 20 years. One wife I spoke with who had been married for 23 years confessed to me that she *still* did not know how much money her husband made! Can you imagine that?

> Couples need to work together and be equally knowledgeable about the financial affairs of the household because they are partners in marriage, not simply two individuals living in the same house.

Partnership in the economic affairs of the home is even more important in our day with more and more women working full-time careers. More families today than ever before have two primary income sources—husband and wife. This calls for both to be up front and open with their income, sharing it in a common pool. Otherwise, they will sow the seeds of division.

Unless we train and condition ourselves differently, it is easy to fall into the "mine and yours" trap: "I work my job, you work yours; I have my money, you have yours. I can do whatever I like with my money, and you can do the same with yours." This kind of attitude will destroy oneness between partners. Remember, there is no "mine" and "yours" in marriage; there is only "ours." Two independent people coming together in marriage do not automatically start thinking as one as soon as the wedding is over. If they enter marriage thinking and acting as one, it is only because they learned how to do it together during their engagement.

There is no room in marriage for division, especially over finances. Ultimately, division will destroy the relationship. Jesus said, "Any kingdom divided against itself will be ruined, and a house divided against itself will fall" (Luke 11:17b). Although Jesus was referring specifically to satan and his kingdom, and to the accusation that He was casting out demons by satan's power, the principle applies equally to any human relationship. Whether it is an engagement "house" or a marriage "house," a house divided against itself will fall.

EDUCATIONAL GOALS

Engagement should also be a time when a couple nails down their personal and professional educational goals and commit themselves to doing everything they can to ensure each other's success in reaching those goals. The ideal is for both partners to complete all of their planned education before getting married, but this is not always possible or practical. In those instances, the couple should try to schedule their wedding in such a way as to cause the least possible impact on educational plans. For example, if the young woman has one year of college left, postpone the wedding for a year. Let her finish her degree. Both she and her fiancé will be better for it and so will their marriage.

Too many couples never attain their educational goals because they underestimate the impact that getting married will have on their lives. Of all the experiences that human beings have between birth and death, nothing is more stressful than getting married. Marriage injects more stress into life than having a baby or experiencing the death of a loved one. By itself, stress is neutral, neither good nor bad. Stress results from any major change in our lives and is the measure of our ability to adjust to those changes. Life changes may be good or bad, but they will create stress either way. Regardless of the source, stress can have profound negative effects on us physiologically, mentally, emotionally, and spiritually.

Normally, marriage is a good life change, yet it generates a significant amount of stress. Many couples who assume they can get married and continue with the same plans they had before become discouraged very quickly when they slam into the brick wall of reality.

Take it from me, in almost every situation it is much more difficult to continue or to finish school after getting married than it is to do so before getting married. I've seen it happen too many times. Young people with a lot of promise, a lot on the ball, and brilliant and wonderful dreams seem headed for the heights of success. Then, while still in school, they get married and everything changes. First the husband drops out in order to earn money so his wife can stay in school. Before long, however, a baby arrives on the scene, and now mamma has to drop out of school to care for it. This couple that once showed such enormous potential is now limping along from month to month on income barely sufficient to meet their expenses. They would like to get better jobs and make more money, but they lack the education to qualify for them. They would like to return to school and get their degree but they cannot afford it. Both are working but neither can quit to go back to school because they need both incomes to stay afloat.

Don't fall into that trap. Careful planning and preparation during the engagement period can help ensure success in reaching a couple's educational goals. If both are still in school and have the means to finish even after getting married, then by all means, they should do it. If not, then they should decide which one will finish school first. That one goes to school while the other one works. After graduation, they switch.

This kind of cooperation and coordination won't happen by accident. Couples must plan for success, and the time for planning is during engagement. Engagement is the time to establish the plan; marriage is the time to work the plan. Start by carefully assessing the situation. How much money will it take it for one to finish school? For both to finish? How long will it take? Can one or both be full-time students or will they have to attend school part time? Are the couple's current resources sufficient to support them on a daily basis as well as pay for school? If not, where will they get the additional financial support they need?

> Couples must plan for success, and the time for planning is during engagement.

These kinds of questions and details are better handled during engagement than during marriage because engagement allows more flexibility while both partners are still technically single. Once they marry, they will then have to allow not only for their own personal needs, desires, and goals, but also for those of the other person. Wise couples, if they can, will work out an educational plan and have it fully in place before they tie the knot so that after they are married they will know exactly where they are going and how they are going to get there.

PARENTING PHILOSOPHY

Another important area for couples to discuss and make preparation for before marriage involves parenting and the whole issue of children. Premarital discussion on this subject should focus on four questions:

- Do we want to have children?
- If so, how many?
- When will we start our family?
- How will we raise and discipline our children?

The relevance of the last three questions depends on how we answer the first one. Obviously, if a couple for some reason chooses not to have children, the other questions don't apply. There could be any number of reasons why a couple might choose not to have any children. Career and professional plans are probably the most frequent reason. Fear of passing on a confirmed hereditary health problem or birth defect is another. Whatever the reason, each couple must decide for themselves.

Most engaged couples look forward to having children. The Bible, and particularly the Old Testament, speaks often of the joys and the blessings as well as the responsibilities of parenthood. Solomon said, "Sons are a heritage from the Lord, children a reward from him. Like arrows in the hands of a warrior are sons born in one's youth. Blessed is the man whose quiver is full of them. They will not be put to shame when they contend with their enemies in the gate" (Ps. 127:3-5). In the beginning, God told Adam and Eve, "Be fruitful and increase in number" (Gen. 1:28b). Couples who choose to have children choose a good thing.

Assuming that a couple chooses to have children, the next question is, "How many?" The answer may come down to a simple matter of economics. When planning for a family, couples need to be down-to-earth and realistic concerning not only the number of children they desire, but how many they can *afford* financially. Let's face it; it costs money to raise a child from infancy to adulthood. Beyond the financial consideration lies the emotional element. Couples need to make a thoroughly honest assessment not only of how many children they can afford to raise, but also how many they can give proper love, attention, and emotional support to. Children are too important and precious for parents to skimp and cut corners on either financially or emotionally.

I have seen too many couples whose heads are filled with spiritual foolishness that says, "It doesn't matter how many kids we have; the Lord will provide." All the while they are trying to raise 10 kids on $1,500.00 a month with another baby on the way. Not only is that foolishness, but it is also irresponsible and presumptuous. It lays the blame on God if the couple cannot support all their children. This very same attitude helps explain why so many children today have been emotionally abandoned at home or literally abandoned on the street.

Deciding how soon to have children depends on the specific circumstances of each couple. Ideally, starting a family should wait until both partners have completed all their formal education and have their careers or professions well-established. Children deserve to be born into a family environment that is emotionally, spiritually, and financially stable.

Discipline of children is another subject related to parenting that couples need to be in clear agreement on. I have seen marriages break up because the husband and wife disagreed on how to discipline their children. This is a difficult area because everyone has his or her own ideas and opinions. Most people discipline their children the way their own parents disciplined them.

Even people who grew up under abusive or neglectful parents and vowed they would never be that way to their own children tend to fall into the same mold, particularly under pressure. It is not surprising that people tend to adopt whatever model they saw at home, even when it is a negative model.

For this reason it is critically important for engaged couples to discuss their backgrounds, models, and philosophies of parenting. They need to understand each other's frame of reference in order to work together in developing the philosophy of discipline that they will use with their own children.

Quite often, the difference centers on the question of corporal punishment. To spank or not to spank—that is the question.

One person says spanking is biblical and therefore appropriate while another person says it is a form of child abuse and should not be used. The Bible does say that the "rod of discipline" is appropriate for children. Some interpret this rod literally as a form of physical punishment, while others view the "rod" figuratively as referring to the firm principle of discipline itself.

> Children deserve to be born into a family environment that is emotionally, spiritually, and financially stable.

Either way, engaged couples need to come to an agreement as to the disciplinary approach they will use so that they can present a united approach to their children. Otherwise, the children will learn very quickly to play one parent against the other. If daddy believes in spanking but mommy doesn't, as soon as daddy takes a belt or a paddle to one of the kids, the child will run to mommy and wail, "Daddy hit me!" and there go mommy and daddy in a big fight. It is important for parents to agree not to disagree in front of the children.

Another parenting-related factor that is an issue for more and more couples is the blended family. If either or both partners have children from a previous relationship who are living with them, both partners need to be in absolute understanding and agreement concerning the authority of the partner who will be in the role of step-parent. At the same time, they must make sure that the children involved understand their relationship to the step-parent and the authority he or she exercises over them.

> Parenting must never be left to chance;
> it is too important a responsibility.

Before a couple steps up to the wedding altar, they should have their parenting philosophy and plan thoroughly worked out and in place. Parenting must never be left to chance; it is too important a responsibility.

SEXUAL STANDARDS

Engagement is a very special period in the life of a couple as they carefully plan their life together and prepare for the day when they become husband and wife. For this very reason, engagement is also a very dangerous time that calls for great caution on their part, particularly with regard to sexual matters. One of the biggest challenges couples face during engagement is the temptation to go too far sexually. As spiritual and emotional intimacy grow in a couple, so too does the desire for physical intimacy. This is perfectly natural, and engaged couples should not fear those feelings or condemn themselves when those feelings arise. At the same time, however, they should exercise great restraint to avoid slipping into sin and immoral behavior.

> One of the biggest challenges couples face during
> engagement is the temptation to go too far sexually.

Many couples underestimate the power of the human sex drive and how easy it is to slide onto the slippery slope of physical arousal. It usually starts very subtly in the mind. The more a couple gets to know each other—the more they talk and dream and share and plan together—the more comfortable and cozy they feel with each other. They share endearments and whisper "sweet nothings" in each other's ear: "I love you." "I love you, too." "I love the way you smile." "You have such beautiful eyes." "I love the smell of your hair." Words are often accompanied by touch. Within certain, very strict limits, physical displays of affection are appropriate and even natural for an engaged couple: holding hands, a warm hug, a good-night kiss. The danger here is that even these simple acts, when combined with the emotional intimacy the couple already shares, can escalate from innocent affection to full-blown petting and beyond. Once on that slippery slope, it is very hard to get off before going too far.

Some people make the mistake of assuming that the giddy, tingly feeling they get when their betrothed touches them is a sign of "true love." They think, "This has to be love. This must be the person for me because I have never felt this way before." Love has nothing to do with it. Oh, true love may be present, but that warm tingly feeling is due not to love but to chemicals. Sexual arousal is a chemical reaction. When certain parts of our bodies are touched, certain enzymes and chemicals that trigger sexual desire are released into our system. The more our bodies are stimulated, the more chemicals are released and the greater our sexual desire grows until it becomes a virtually unstoppable flood.

Bearing this in mind, it is vital that engaged couples be in total agreement with each other on the standards they will follow with regard to sexual activity and expression. For Christian couples, this means that anything beyond innocent tender affection is off-limits, including especially heavy petting and sexual intercourse of any kind. Sex is a special kind of intimacy that is properly reserved exclusively for a man and a woman who have entered into a committed marriage relationship.

People who feel strongly about each other want to be close to each other. It is perfectly natural to want to show affection for someone we care about. Showing affection is a good thing, but it comes more easily to some people than to others. Children who grow up in affectionate families where the parents were very open with their touching and tenderness tend to become the same way. They learn that affection is very natural and non-sexual, and become very relaxed and comfortable with it. Even as adults, they can handle affection without always relating it to sex.

On the other hand, people from non-affectionate homes and who saw little or no open expressions of love often have trouble as adults dealing with affection. Once they begin to experience physical desire and arousal, they easily (but erroneously) conclude that it must be love because they have never felt anything like it before. Someone in this situation who also is already starved for affection has few defenses to guard him or her against giving into those desires and going all the way.

Most people go into a relationship with some kind of standard, some silent unspoken line they will not cross with regard to sex. This standard may come from the person's spiritual beliefs and upbringing or it may come from cultural pressure and norms. For Christians, it may be their spiritual conscience, the Holy Spirit within them convicting and guiding them as to how far they should go.

> The fact that a couple is getting married does not justify or excuse premature and improper sexual behavior.

Many times, when a couple enters the engagement period, something happens to this standard. The two of them tend to become more lenient with their behavior and go farther physically with each other than they ever have before. Because they are engaged, they drop their defenses a little bit more, thinking, "What's the difference? We're getting married anyway." The fact that a couple is getting married does not justify or excuse premature and improper sexual behavior.

This is why it is so important for engaged couples to commit themselves to a standard of absolute sexual purity before marriage. Failure in this area affects not just the body, but also the spirit. Paul's words to the Corinthian believers are as fresh and timely for us today as they were 2,000 years ago:

> *Flee from sexual immorality. All other sins a man commits are outside his body, but he who sins sexually sins against his own body. Do you not know that your body is a temple of the Holy Spirit, who is in you, whom you have received from God? You are not your own; you were bought at a price. Therefore honor God with your body* (1 Cor. 6:18-20).

Engagement is the period where a couple's sexual standards either stand or fall because it is during engagement that those standards face their greatest test. By successfully handling sexual temptation, a couple proves their maturity, integrity, faithfulness, and self-control.

In our day and age, more than ever, young men and women need to learn to appreciate and value the sanctity of their virginity. One of the greatest gifts any person can give his or her marriage partner on their wedding day is a body that is sexually pure, because then they can enjoy an intimacy they have never shared with anyone else.

> By successfully handling sexual temptation, a couple proves their maturity, integrity, faithfulness, and self-control.

What if it's too late? What about those people who have lost their virginity? Have they no hope of ever enjoying the rich intimacy of a committed and pure marriage relationship? With Jesus there is always hope. Jesus is able not only to forgive our sins but also to cleanse our conscience. He can supernaturally restore a lost virginity in the spiritual and moral sense so that a person can enter a committed marriage relationship free of guilt and shame. The writer of Hebrews says, "How much more, then, will the blood of Christ, who through the eternal Spirit offered himself unblemished to God, cleanse our consciences from acts that lead to death, so that we may serve the living God!" (Heb. 9:14).

When our sins are forgiven, the Bible says that we are "justified," which is a legal term that, in laymen's terms, means "just as if I'd" never sinned. Spiritually and morally we are made new, just as if our sin never existed. This newness includes the sexual realm as well. The blood of Jesus can free a man or woman from their guilty conscience so they can stand before a minister and get married, and nobody can point a finger at them and accuse them because Jesus has made them free. He gave them their virginity back, and that is something only Christ can do.

Engagement is where Christian couples prove their standards, and that is why engagement is so important. A couple demonstrates their faithfulness to each other by staying true and remaining pure even during a time when it is easy to become lax and drop their guard. If they can maintain their standards during this critical period, it will strengthen their confidence that they will maintain their standards into and throughout their marriage, remaining faithful both to themselves and to each other.

Betrothed couples should not take their engagement lightly. Engagement is the time when all the seeds for future marital success are planted. The degree of success and happiness that they experience in their marriage may be directly related to the effectiveness of the preparations they make during their engagement. Redeeming the time during engagement—using that time wisely—will help ensure a marriage that is fruitful, reaches its fullest potential, and enjoys the blessings of God.

CHAPTER SIX

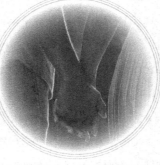

PRINCIPLES

1. Engagement is hard-core planning, in which a couple gets down to the brass tacks of preparing for life after the wedding.

2. Every believing couple should lay a strong, solid, spiritual foundation for their marriage during their engagement.

3. Spiritual harmony promotes oneness, which is one vital characteristic couples should develop during their engagement.

4. Long before they say "I do," couples should discuss and nail down the financial strategy they will take into their marriage.

5. Careful planning and preparation during the engagement period can help ensure success in reaching a couple's educational goals.

6. Before a couple steps up to the wedding altar, they should have their parenting philosophy and plan thoroughly worked out and in place.

7. It is vitally important for engaged couples to commit themselves to a standard of absolute sexual purity before marriage.

8. Engagement is where Christian couples prove their standards, which is why engagement is so important.

9. Engagement is the time when all the seeds for future marital success are planted.

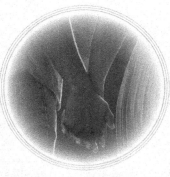

REFLECTIONS

CHAPTER ONE REFLECTIONS

CHAPTER TWO REFLECTIONS

CHAPTER THREE REFLECTIONS

CHAPTER FOUR REFLECTIONS

CHAPTER FIVE REFLECTIONS

CHAPTER SIX REFLECTIONS

ABOUT THE AUTHOR

Dr. Myles Munroe was a beloved statesman and internationally renowned bestselling author, lecturer, life coach, and government consultant. His legacy continues to impact countless lives—individually launching people into lives of discovered purpose and unlocked potential, and corporately ushering the global church into a greater revelation of demonstrating the Kingdom of God. He, along with his wife, Ruth Ann, served as senior pastors of Bahamas Faith Ministries International Fellowship. They have two children, Charisa and Chairo.